LOST
EVANSVILLE

LOST
EVANSVILLE

JAMES LACHLAN MACLEOD

THE
History
PRESS

Published by The History Press
Charleston, SC
www.historypress.com

First published 2023

Manufactured in the United States

ISBN 9781467153324

Library of Congress Control Number: 2023938436

Notice: The information in this book is true and complete to the best of our knowledge. It is offered without guarantee on the part of the author or The History Press. The author and The History Press disclaim all liability in connection with the use of this book.

For Jess, Eilidh, Calum and Gavin, with all my love

Dedicated to the working men and women of Evansville, who built this city

CONTENTS

ACKNOWLEDGEMENTS

None of the work that I have done as an Evansville historian would have been possible without the warm and gracious welcome given to me by the people here involved in the field. From the beginning, the local historians in this community have treated me not like an ignorant alien but as a friend and a colleague. They were always more than willing to provide information, suggestions and insight, not to mention great company. I will always appreciate these gifts. Among many others, I want to thank Tom Lonnberg, Bill Bartelt, Terry Hughes, Kelley Coures, Amber Gowen, Jon Carl, Pat Sides, Rob Spear, Stan Schmitt, Dennis Au, Joe Engler, Greg Hager, Chris Cooke, Pat Wathen, Stella Ress, Steve Appel, Denise Lynn, Mike Linderman, Tory Schendel-Vyvoda and Jennifer Greene.

I greatly appreciate the hard work of the many local archivists and librarians who protect and preserve the record of our past. The Evansville Vanderburgh Public Library, the Willard Library, the University of Evansville Library, the Evansville Museum of Arts, History & Science, the Evansville African American Museum, the Vanderburgh County Clerk's Archive and the University of Southern Indiana Library made this research possible. Josh Bowlds was a remarkable research assistant who provided me with invaluable help, and I also want to acknowledge the research funding received from the Southwestern Indiana Historical Society, the Vanderburgh County Historical Society and an Arts, Research, and Teaching Grant from the University of Evansville.

I am extremely grateful to Bill Bartelt, Jon Carl, Kelley Coures, Joe Engler, Terry Hughes, Tom Lonnberg and Watez Phelps, who read and improved parts of the text. I also greatly appreciate the help I received from John Rodrigue, acquisitions editor at The History Press, and all the editorial staff there. Any errors of interpretation or fact in this work are my responsibility.

Most of all, I want to thank my family, who have tolerated and encouraged this project over the past few years as we lived through a global pandemic. This book is for you.

ABBREVIATIONS

Used in Notes and Captions

EA: *Evansville Argus*

EAAM: Evansville African American Museum

EC: *Evansville Courier*

ECP: *Evansville Courier and Press*

EDJ: *Evansville Daily Journal*

EE: *Evansville Examiner*

EJ: *Evansville Journal*

EJN: *Evansville Journal-News*

EP: *Evansville Press*

EVPL: Evansville Vanderburgh Public Library

GS/LPC/S: George Skadding/The LIFE Picture Collection/Shutterstock

IGWS/IU: Indiana Geological and Water Survey, Indiana University

ISL: Indiana State Library

IUMAA: Indiana University Museum of Archaeology and Anthropology and the Trustees of Indiana University.

LOC: Library of Congress

MI: Mapping Inequality: Redlining in New Deal America

SCP: *Sunday Courier and Press*

UoE: University of Evansville Archives

USI: University of Southern Indiana Rice Library

WL: Willard Library

INTRODUCTION

Americans have…moved forward allowing little of the past to encumber their motion. Although historical events were duly recorded, the buildings, the most tangible expression of the American heritage, were considered irrelevant to progress, hence expendable. Buildings were often regarded as obsolete prematurely and were replaced or "face lifted" with materials of little enduring character. In more recent times, old buildings have been allowed to decay until eventually demolished, leaving asphalt parking lots or empty waste lands. [1]

These words of Evansville historic preservationist Joan Marchand are an elegant statement of the challenges faced by those who want to preserve the past, both material and cultural. Like every other city in the world, much of Evansville's past has been lost. Although the city had its origins in 1812 when a man named Hugh McGary Jr. purchased 440.8 acres on land at a bend on the Ohio River and built a log cabin, the oldest remaining building in that part of the city today is thought to be the Stockwell-Wheeler double house on SE First Street, which was built a quarter century later. [2] The 1827 Kenyon House is closer to Newburgh, and there are a handful of other antebellum structures dotted around, but nothing at all remains of the city that grew up between 1812 and the 1830s. While a number of fine nineteenth- and early twentieth-century structures remain, much of the material culture from that period is gone. The ongoing process of material destruction continues; as recently as 2021, one of Evansville's most significant structures of the mid-twentieth century—the

The former Faultless Caster facility burns, December 2022. *James MacLeod.*

Old National Bank building at 420 Main, the city's tallest building when it was completed in 1970—was dramatically imploded.[3] In late 2022, not one but two of the city's most historic industrial sites were lost when first much of the Hercules/Servel factory and then the Faultless Caster facility burned to the ground. And it is not just the physical structures—many of the city's memories, substantial parts of its history, have been lost too.

Lost Evansville seeks to tell the story of a midwestern city that was significantly affected by the upheavals of the period from the end of World War II to the 1970s. During a period of immense social, cultural, political and economic change in the country at large, Evansville underwent a transformation as the wartime factories were closed, iconic companies moved away, the old downtown was largely replaced by new structures, road-building projects cut apart traditional neighborhoods and the Black community fought doggedly for its civil rights. All these issues raised huge challenges and opened up opportunities—and they profoundly shaped the city that we see today. There was much that was lost, but it is important to stress that this is also a story of what came in its place and what was preserved against the odds; the physical marks of 1945–75 are all around and are impossible to miss. The main roads that move traffic through the city, the nature of the downtown, the skyline, the older suburbs, the ethnic makeup of the city's schools, the presence of two universities and the physical heart of city and county governments—these are just a few of the powerful visual reminders of the permanent changes that were made in Evansville during the most profoundly significant thirty-year period in the city's two-hundred-year history.

What makes this period in Evansville so interesting is that the city's experience at the time is both a reflection of wider processes that were going on in the United States and a unique case study of a particular local set of circumstances. The American economy was shifting, transportation was changing, urban landscapes were being transformed, women and minorities were claiming their rights, racial conflict was intense and wars were being fought—all of these had profound effects on Evansville, as they did almost everywhere else. Urban renewal, involving as it did the destruction of people's homes and the obliteration of old neighborhoods, happened all over the United States, and the civil rights movement was an ongoing national phenomenon. Furthermore, the business shifts that changed Evansville were happening across the country as companies moved out of old factories and offices in older industrial towns and cities to new locations with new facilities in the West and the South.[4] But the Evansville story is also unique, given the specific set of people, locations, businesses, beliefs, traditions, ethnicities and pressures present here.

After the first chapter outlines the earlier history of Evansville—much of it lost history—chapter 2 looks at the dramatic production boom that happened during World War II and how the factories that fueled the boom virtually disappeared, along with the memory of what was done in the city. The Evansville Shipyard, the Republic Aviation factory, the Evansville Ordnance plant and dozens of other plants answered the call to help win the war but were then quickly gone or repurposed—sometimes with breathtaking speed.[5] Huge federal housing projects were emptied and in most cases completely demolished, leaving little evidence that they had ever existed, and thousands of migrant workers left the city, often taking the stories of what happened here in the war with them. The next part of this chapter focuses on the postwar economy, which is an area that perhaps exhibits the positives and negatives of the era more than any other. It is also an area around which several myths persist that need to be addressed, including the one that Evansville's biggest challenge was militant labor unions.[6]

Part of the reason that the economy survived and confidence revived in this period is that there was an extensive amount of infrastructure investment and construction, and the remarkable physical transformation of Evansville is the focus of chapter 3.[7] It was a time of enormous gains and enormous losses, and as one local writer put it in 1965, "The status quo is a thing of the past in Evansville as destruction of the old and construction of the new brings many changes across the face of our city."[8] The changes were multifaceted and often interconnected and overlapping, but for clarity they are analyzed in this chapter as four major areas: housing, urban renewal, roads and public buildings.

The fourth chapter focuses on social change in Evansville over the course of these decades but centered on the 1960s and '70s. Given the centrality of race in American history and the fact that this has been in many ways a lost aspect of the Evansville story, the main focus of chapter 4 is race. Starting with a brief history of racism in the city, the chapter analyzes four aspects of the racial politics of the era that were significant in Evansville: violence and its effects, the struggle for school integration, the desegregation of public life and the fight against segregation in housing.

Before discussing all of these issues, however, a substantial foundation has to be laid. Everything that happened in Evansville between 1945 and 1975 was built on what came before, and it is with the origins and early history of the city that this book starts.

1

People have lived around the area we now call Evansville for at least one thousand years. Indeed, one of the country's greatest historical sites is in Evansville, and it is a potent symbol of both loss and preservation. Thriving between 1000 and 1450 CE the site that is now called Angel Mounds was a center of a chiefdom in the Mississippian Indian civilization, and the area covered over one hundred acres. It was a palisaded town of around two hundred houses and featured eleven earthen mounds on mostly flat land located close to the Ohio River. It was a significant site—the historian James Madison has called it "the largest, most complex Mississippian village in Indiana," but all human settlement there seems to have ended about 1450, probably due to the depletion of resources.[9] In some ways, it was both the "first Evansville" and the first "lost Evansville"—one historian called it "the historical antecedent of Evansville," while another observed, "It remained unnoticed by explorers, surveyors and settlers and there was no mention made of it until 1876 in descriptive or historical accounts."[10] Historians and archaeologists know much about the site, but what is known is just a fraction of the story—although millions of artifacts have been recovered from the site, only a tiny percentage of the area has been excavated.

Much—indeed most—has been lost, but what has been discovered and preserved is remarkable. Angel Mounds was first excavated between 1939 and 1942, mostly with labor provided by the U.S. Works Progress Administration, directed by Glenn A. Black, a prominent archaeologist from

WPA excavations at Angel Mounds, 1940. *IUMAA.*

Indiana University.[11] Under the oversight of the Indiana Department of Natural Resources and the Indiana Historical Society, the work continued throughout the 1950s, and although it was affected by Dr Black's death in 1964, it persisted and the site continues to be used as an outdoor laboratory by archaeologists in the present day.[12] The site came under the control of Indiana University after Glenn Black's death, and by the late 1960s, over 2.5 million artifacts had been excavated. Black's old friend, the pharmaceutical executive and philanthropist Eli Lilly, helped pay for the interpretive center that is still at Angel Mounds today—that building was opened in 1972, although it has been subsequently updated several times.[13] Although it is today one of Evansville's historical jewels, one that preserves and tells the story of the past in a captivating, evolving and systematic way, it is worth noting that the story might not have ended that way. In 1964, consultant F. Elwood Allen, hired by the city at the cost of $10,000, astonishingly proposed building a golf course at Angel Mounds. It was still being discussed by the Park Board in 1967 and 1968, and the terribly bad idea did not finally die until 1970.[14] Sometimes the margin between history being saved and being lost is extremely fine.

The arrival of Europeans brought a new chapter to the history of this region, and the modern history of Evansville began with Hugh McGary buying land at the horseshoe bend of the Ohio River. He quickly established two licensed ferries and called his location McGary's Landing.[15] In 1814, the community was named Evansville after McGary's friend Colonel Robert M. Evans, and it was originally the county seat for Warrick County. In January 1818, a new county, Vanderburgh, was created out of parts of Warrick and Posey Counties, with Evansville as its seat. A circuit court convened there the very next month, albeit in Hugh McGary's own home; he was also the clerk of the court.[16] Indiana became a state in 1816, and in 1818, a charter from the state legislature made Evansville a town; that year, the community's first election had twenty-five voters. By 1819, a census revealed that the town had no fewer than one hundred residents and there was, almost inevitably, a tavern.[17] A branch of the state Bank of Indiana was established in 1834 as the town's first bank, and this undoubtedly stimulated economic confidence and development. There were ups and downs over the next three decades, but on January 28, 1847, Evansville was chartered as a city. "The city," wrote historian Robert Patry, "covered about 280 acres and had about 3,000 people. The property in Evansville was valued at just under one million dollars."[18] It was the eighth-largest city in Indiana. Evansville had arrived on the scene, and in 1857, it absorbed the neighboring city of Lamasco, which had been established to the west in 1836.

It was in this period that the great unfulfilled potential of the Wabash and Erie Canal affected Evansville the most. In an era before the railroad, canals were the dominant transportation infrastructure, and this was to be a super-canal, linking Lake Erie to the Ohio River. News arrived in 1834 that the southern terminus of the canal was to be in Evansville, and as James Morlock put it, "The effect of this news was electrifying. Some believed Evansville would become the largest and most important city west of the Appalachian.…The promise of the canal seemed to predict a bright future for this locality."[19] Indeed, pioneering local historian Darrel Bigham argued that Evansville's "takeoff" was mainly because of hopes based on the canal.[20] The canal was a gigantic undertaking—459 miles long from Toledo, Ohio, to Evansville, the longest canal ever built in the United States. Built mostly by Irish laborers, the canal was unfortunately dogged by political struggles and a financial crisis that crippled much of the country and bankrupted the State of Indiana. Irishmen who had fled famine at home perished in their hundreds from cholera. The canal was finally completed in 1853, but it continued to be beset by problems caused by shoddy construction, droughts, freezing, flooding and burrowing muskrats. Most importantly, by the time it was completed, the railroad had arrived; a new era was dawning, and

The Founding of Evansville by Hugh McGary ~ 1817

Karl Kae Knecht's drawing of Hugh McGary's arrival. *EVPL.*

the age of the canal was all but over. "And in the end," wrote Evansville columnist Joe Aaron in 2009, "after all the millions had been spent and the state was virtually bankrupt, after cholera had swept across the land to fell hundreds of workmen in their tracks—it became perhaps the costliest fiasco in Indiana history, a bother and an eyesore, and a perennial breeder of malaria."[21]

The Wabash and Erie Canal in the Evansville area is a fine example of lost history—a story of lost money, lost lives and lost potential whose physical evidence has been all but lost. One writer remarked in 1974, "Today, one driving on Fifth Street in Evansville might be surprised to know that he is traveling on a thoroughfare built on the bed of the old and historic Wabash and Erie Canal....The driver will see no remaining evidence along the way to remind him that this canal ever existed."[22] There are historical markers here and there, and those who know where to look can point out Evansville's remaining remnants of the canal, but it is largely forgotten.[23] As Mike Burns of the *Courier* wrote in 1967, "The noisy revelry of construction gangs, the shouted orders as towboats docked in downtown Evansville, and the steady gait of strong mules as they pulled crammed towboats through the quiet countryside have dissolved into history. They are memories of a forgotten promise that was never fulfilled."[24]

Before the canal was even completed, the first railway locomotive had been delivered to Evansville, and this seventeen-ton English-made machine symbolized the modern world's arrival in the city—and perhaps the city's arrival in the modern world. The second half of the nineteenth century, in contrast to the era of the canal debacle, was a period when Evansville's promise certainly was fulfilled. And while much of this period is also lost history, there are significant parts of it that survive, both physically and institutionally. The *Evansville Courier*'s first edition was printed on January 7, 1845, as a weekly, and it is still published, almost 180 years later, as the city's only remaining daily newspaper.[25] The first public library was established around 1848 with the books located in the office of the county auditor, and the Evansville Library Association was incorporated in 1855. In 1884, its collection of 8,717 volumes became the starting point for the Willard Library, a gift to the city from the philanthropist Willard Carpenter that opened to the public—of all races—in 1885 and has been serving the city ever since.[26] As the *Press* observed in 1965, "In these times of great change in our city, it is comforting now and then to see something remain stable and unscathed through the years....The structure remains basically in appearance today as it did at dedication

Wabash and Erie Canal historic marker on the Old Courthouse lawn. *James MacLeod.*

ceremonies in the spring of 1884."[27] The building remains much the same today, albeit with a tasteful extension. The public library system thrived; in 1913, two branch libraries financed by Scottish philanthropist Andrew Carnegie were dedicated, and a year later, more Carnegie money allowed the opening of the Cherry Branch Library for the African American population. Two of these buildings are still in use as libraries, part of a flourishing public library system, while the African American library building is lost to history; it was sold in 1955 and demolished in the 1970s to allow Welborn Hospital expansion.[28]

As with any community, religion played a significant role in Evansville from almost the very beginning. The first organized service was held in Hugh McGary's warehouse in 1819, and the first permanent church in what is now Evansville—the presbyterian "Little Church on the Hill"—was built in 1832. A plaque on Main Street marks the approximate spot. The Old North United Methodist Church chapel, built in 1832 as a nondenominational meetinghouse, is one of the oldest buildings still standing in Vanderburgh County and is in Evansville today, but when built, it was in a community known as Mechanicsville that was separate from Evansville itself.[29] Over time, as people settled in the community and wealth grew, more buildings were erected for the purpose of worship. Immigration brought people of different religious viewpoints, most notably Catholics, Protestants and Jews; these groups were themselves further divided by ethnicity and precise religious perspective. By the middle of the century, religious groups were feeling confident and wealthy enough to erect significant buildings, and this period is Evansville's golden age of religious architecture. The first Jewish temple was the B'nai Israel, built in 1864 but razed in the early twentieth century. Many beautiful church buildings have been lost over the years, but some of the most impressive old churches in the city date to the second half of the nineteenth century. The 1860s brought Trinity United Methodist and Liberty Baptist, both wonderful historic treasures that are with us still, as well as St. Mary's Catholic downtown, the oldest remaining Catholic church in the city. Grace Presbyterian Church (now First Presbyterian) was built in the 1870s, and then in the 1880s came the iconic twin spires of St. Boniface Catholic Church on the West Side and the impressive lines of St Paul's Episcopal downtown.[30]

Education was another area that saw significant growth in this period, and by 1910, Evansville historian Frank M. Gilbert could gush,

> *Evansville may well be called a city of schools.…In perhaps no other city of the same proportion of population, are there so many beautiful buildings of such great magnitude equipped with the very best facilities for instruction and where the…children could obtain as good an education in every respect* [as] *in any city in the world.*[31]

First Presbyterian Church. *EVPL*.

Hyperbole aside, it is clearly true that education was a high priority in Evansville in the second half of the nineteenth century, and while many of the key original buildings are lost, the ongoing importance of educational institutions to the city is still evident. Although there were some rough log-built schools in the area before it, the first brick schoolhouse in Evansville was a small building at Third and Main, built in 1821.[32] At this time, all schools were private, and the first public school was not erected until 1855, when the "Public School" opened on Mulberry Street. The school was

Central High School. *EVPL.*

subsequently known as Canal School, Mulberry School and, after 1915, Wheeler School, and it served the city until 1972. It was closed and sold to Welborn Baptist Hospital that year and demolished in 1974.[33] Carpenter School, the second public grade school, opened in 1860, closed in 1957 and was razed in 1961 in what the *Evansville Press* termed "the final step in the 27-block High Street slum clearance program."[34] The first public high school in the city was located initially in the Canal School, but a large purpose-built structure was erected in 1868 on Seventh Street. It was called Evansville High School until a second public high school, Francis Joseph Reitz, opened on the West Side in 1918; thereafter it was known as Central High School.[35] An ornate and beautiful structure with a magnificent clock tower, it was vacated in 1971 and demolished in 1973. The only building of the campus that remains is the gymnasium, which was opened in 1927. And although not located in Evansville, the college that would in 1919 become Evansville College also dates from this era—Moores Hill Male and Female Collegiate Institute was founded in 1854 in Dearborn County, Indiana. At that time, there were only four other coeducational institutions in the United States, and it was the first in Indiana.[36]

This era, a time of commercial success for the city, saw some grand public architecture begin to grace the streets. Again, although many are now lost,

Old Courthouse. *EVPL.*

some of these mid-nineteenth-century buildings are still standing and still add elegance to the city. Most striking of these structures is the building known today as the Old Courthouse, built from 1888 to 1890 on the site of the old Wabash and Erie Canal basin. It replaced the earlier structure that was erected on the northwest corner of Third and Main Streets in 1857. The 1857 courthouse replaced the first purpose-built courthouse, which was erected on the southeast corner of Third and Main in 1820.[37] The Old Courthouse is probably the finest Victorian-era building in Evansville, and it was breathlessly praised in a front-page article in the *Courier* upon its completion in 1890:

> *An architectural triumph. Kingdoms may fall, dynasties change, or republics become no more, but only an upheaval of the earth or an unlooked for phenomenon of nature can obliterate that perpetual monument of Vanderburgh's greatness, the new county court house. Majestic in its solidity, grand in its sublimity, it will remain an everlasting record of the handiwork*

of Nineteenth Century architects and artisans, a fitting memorial to the enterprise of the men who financiered the affairs of this county, long after their names are forgotten.[38]

Eighty-eight years later, Louisville-based architectural critic William Morgan observed, "There are not a few states that would be happy to have this incredible limestone, Neo-Baroque, triple-domed monumental pile as their state capitol."[39] It was all a far cry from the city's humble origins.

There are two other outstanding public buildings from this period that are still standing. One of these is the County Jail and Sheriff's Residence opposite the Old Courthouse, completed in 1890 and described at the time as "a magnificent work…one of the handsomest ornaments in an architectural way among the public buildings in this city."[40] Rendered surplus to requirements in 1969, it lived a precarious life before being repurposed as an office space, which it remains today. The second example is the U.S. Post Office, Courthouse and Custom House on NW Second Street, erected between 1875 and 1879, of which the city's historic preservation staff said in 1981, "Conceived in the electric atmosphere of post-war national growth and spending, the Old Post Office was a symbol of the federal government's omniscient presence and the hegemony of Evansville in matters of trade and commerce."[41] It is an excellent example of "Ruskinian Gothic" architecture, and despite many challenges since its role was superseded by the new federal building in 1969, it remains today a vibrant part of a revitalized downtown.[42]

This was also the period that saw the United States torn apart by the Civil War, with Evansville standing on the front lines of that great conflict and on the fault line that divided North and South. Local men enlisted in twenty-six different Federal regiments while others, pulled by different loyalties, fought for the South. This at times literally pitted brother against brother—the McCutchan family of McCutchanville saw Marcus fighting in the Confederate Twenty-Seventh Tennessee Infantry against Union troops including his brother Charles at the Battle of Shiloh.[43] In June 1861, Evansville was gripped by war fever as news arrived that six hundred Confederates were on their way to attack the city; a unit of home guards and enlisted men responded but "returned the following morning when it failed to find the alleged attackers."[44] It all seemed, perhaps, a thrilling adventure, but as James Madison observed about Indiana generally, "The war that seemed so romantic and glorious at the outset gradually came to be understood for what it was—the grimmest and most difficult collective experience Americans had yet faced."[45] For Evansville, the grim

Nine-year-old Union army drummer boy John W. Messick of Evansville. *USI.*

reality was evident by October 1861 when the first local men's bodies came home for burial. A crowd as large as thirteen thousand witnessed the funerals of Major John Smith Gavitt and Private Charles McLain in the city; both men died in Missouri at the Battle of Fredericktown, with Gavitt said to be the first Indiana officer to be killed in action.[46] Prisoners of war were brought to the city, and hundreds of wounded men died in hospitals here. In Oak Hill Cemetery, itself a magnificent and unspoiled remnant of the city's past, there are hundreds of Civil War graves: five hundred Union dead, ninety-eight locals and twenty-four Confederate soldiers are buried there in three different sections.[47] Given Evansville's location, it is not surprising that the cemetery contains both Confederate and U.S. memorials, each with a standing soldier statue; the Confederate statue was erected in 1904 and the Union one in 1909.[48]

The period of the late nineteenth and early twentieth centuries was when a relatively new city grew into one that in many ways dominated the region; it was now the second-largest city in Indiana.[49] Historian Darrel Bigham eloquently summarized Evansville's situation around 1900:

> *Through the Ohio and its tributaries…as well as the numerous railroads linking the city to the region, Evansville products like plows, stoves, cigars, flour, and furniture, were well known throughout the lower Midwest and the upper South. Rail links to the growing national urban market, moreover, brought Evansville brand-name goods…to consumers hundreds of miles away.…Unlike its urban neighbors on the lower Ohio, moreover, its economy was not dependent on one or two products, but was relatively diverse.[50]*

The keys to the city's economic success included a strategic location on one of North America's great waterways; abundant natural resources such as fertile land, coal and lumber; and a growing population bolstered by three major waves of immigration—Germans first in the 1840s and again in the 1880s and African Americans after the conclusion of the Civil War. The presence of coal was a huge advantage for Evansville, and eventually millions of bushels of coal were extracted from as many as ten mines inside the city. Reitz Hill was for a long time known as Coal Mine Hill due to the Ingleside mine located there, and the Sunnyside mine's extensive underground tunnels still exist under large portions of Mesker Park and Helfrich Hills golf course.[51] The fertile soil and productive farmlands allowed the city to develop eleven flour mills and gristmills by 1890, and by 1901, there were sixteen incorporated furniture factories turning the abundant local lumber—especially hardwood—into much-desired products.[52] One of these furniture companies, founded by a German immigrant named Albert F. Karges in 1886, ended up as the very last furniture factory in the city before finally closing its doors in 2014.[53] The mid- to late nineteenth-century influx of Germans also saw the growth of what was to become another major Evansville industry—the brewing of beer. Brewing in the city started initially with small local breweries scattered across mostly the West Side, but it almost all eventually coalesced into two huge breweries by the end of the century: the Evansville Brewing Association (later Sterling) and Cook. Once huge enterprises with enormous buildings, virtually nothing remains of all that today.[54] In addition, farm tools, ploughs, bricks and stoves were all Evansville staples at this time, and the economic success was reflected in the city's homes. "The residence portions of the city," boasted a marketing publication in 1895, "are homelike and attractive. The Streets are level and straight, paved with brick, and regularly sprinkled and swept."[55]

The Reitz home on SE First Street. *EVPL.*

There were indeed many beautiful streets, but the fact that many of Evansville's most impressive buildings from this period that still stand today were private houses is a powerful symbol of how much of the wealth generated in the city went into the hands of relatively few families. When walking the Riverside Historic District today, for example, the magnificently lavish houses there are still known by the family names of the members of the elite who owned them—Viele, Reitz, Babcock, Sweetser, Von Behren, Eichel, Venneman and many others.[56] Yet it would be a huge mistake to assume that this wealth was evenly distributed or to imagine that most people lived their lives in homes like these. The poor parts of the city were as dilapidated as the rich parts were opulent.[57] In 1913, the city housing inspector identified several areas of substandard housing, including the neighborhood known as Jimtown and the area of shacks on Pigeon Creek. Of the former it was said, "After inspecting this section one must marvel how people can live with such utter disregard for cleanliness and proper disposal of wastes," and of the latter,

The so-called squatter settlements on the river bank and along Pigeon creek on the West Side are the source of great annoyance both to the police and health departments. Here a large class of poor white people live in squalor and crime. Interned shanty boats, one room shacks, and tents are their dwellings throughout the year.[58]

It is fitting then that one of Evansville's most famous citizens, Albion Fellows Bacon (1865–1933), was a social activist whose remarkably effective life's work was housing reform.

One observer in the early twentieth century said that Indiana's housing legislation was "truly the work of one woman"—Bacon.[59] The stimulus for this passion was the low-quality housing for poor people that she encountered in her home city. In her memoir, *Beauty for Ashes*, she recounted a visit to one of Evansville's tenements, St. Mary's on West Ohio Street, around 1890:

Many of the beds had no sheets, only a filthy ticking; on some lay a sick child, with flies thick upon its face. Old clothing lay about in piles, or hung from large nails driven into the cracked plastering. Not one line or spot of beauty was there in all that mass of hopeless ugliness....Children swarmed in and out, men and women put their heads in at the door, heavy feet passed noisily down the corridor; boys fought on the stairway; old hags scolded, babies cried. To think of living amid all that![60]

Albion Fellows Bacon. *USI.*

Even more striking was a speech she delivered almost two decades later to the Indiana State Conference of Charities and Correction at South Bend in October 1908, in which she said, "We find people infesting the rear premises of our wholesale district, like vermin amid the filth. Sometimes they share a stable with horses or mules. There they have foul air, no water, none of the decencies of living."[61] This, it will be remembered, was in a city that was enjoying enormous economic success and whose commerce and industry dominated the surrounding region. Clearly the fruits of this success were not being equally distributed.

And much of what Bacon was talking about was white Evansville. For Black people in the city, the situation was often even worse. In the judgment of Darrel Bigham, the preeminent historian of Black life in Evansville, "Well before 1900 the physical and institutional ghetto was established, with blacks mired in the least desirable jobs, trapped in residential enclaves, and chained to a pattern of propertylessness, illiteracy, and high mortality and crime rates." By 1900, over 50 percent of the Black population lived in an area around Lincoln Avenue and Eighth and Canal Streets, known popularly as Baptistown, and the area was served by a growing number of all-Black schools (separate and unequal) and churches.[62] Housing conditions were often very poor, and the "dilapidated structures generally had no connection to city sewers and most still relied on cisterns for their water supply."[63] In 1904, the quality of housing on Church Street in Baptistown was so low that most homes were condemned by the fire chief, who also served as the city building inspector.[64] "Life," said Bigham, "was harsh for most blacks,"[65] and in 1909 a local minister declared,

Many of the houses in Baptistown, by their lack of sanitary equipment and their accumulated filth are a menace to the health of the district and, indirectly, to the whole city....The quarter is full of tuberculosis. The disease cannot be escaped when men and women and children herd together in close, dirty rooms. The situation presented by the Baptistown hovel of two rooms, with a family living in each room, is worse than the tenement situation.[66]

A Lewis Wickes Hine photo of child workers in Evansville, 1908. *LOC.*

To make a bad situation for Black people in Evansville worse, the 1920s was also the time of the resurgence of the Ku Klux Klan, and this time one of its centers was Indiana; according to James Madison, "The organization was as strong there as any other state." Probably about 25 percent of all Indiana's native-born white men joined the organization, which at that time was as anti-Catholic as it was anti-Black.[67] And one of its Indiana centers was certainly Evansville, given the connections of the city to key Klan figures like Joe Huffington and D.C. Stephenson. Longtime local journalist, editor and newspaper executive J.C. Kerlin recalled in a 1974 interview,

> *My impression at the time* [is] *that the power of the Klan…was spawned right here in Evansville because D.C. Stephenson, who is the best remembered of all the big time officials, emerged as a Klan leader in Evansville. His palace guard was composed of Evansville men, Evansville people. His lieutenant here who was very, very capable as an administrator, as a leader, as a politician was Joe Huffington.*[68]

Stephenson ultimately became the Klan's leader in Indiana and was briefly one of the most powerful men in the state. An early Klan speaker in Evansville was Caleb Ridley, a Georgia pastor, who addressed over six hundred people, mostly young men, at Evans Hall in September 1921, claiming that there were already hundreds of members in Evansville.[69] In

THE EVANSVILLE JOURNAL—WEDNESDAY, JULY 16, 1924.

(PAID ADVERTISEMENT)

The Knights of the Ku Klux Klan
Evansville Klan No. 1, Realm of Indiana

will hold a public meeting at the
COLISEUM

Thursday Night, July 17th, 1924—7:30 P. M.
EYERYBODY INVITED

Do you know what the Klan stands for Nationally?

Do you know what the Klan stands for in Evansville?

Do you know the Klan's stand politically?

Do you know who we will support?

Do you know who we are?

Do you discuss the Klan from an ignorant or informed viewpoint?

Do you know what makes the Klan the theme of the hour?

☞ A Speaker of National repute will give an address on the Klan and its intentions ☜

Joe M. Huffington of Evansville, Nationally known Klan Leader, will discuss the Klan from a local viewpoint

"Here Yesterday, Here Today, Here Forever"

Full-page newspaper advertisement for a Klan rally, 1924. *EVPL.*

1923, a Mesker Park Klan rally attracted ten thousand people, and in July 1924, the same number attended a rally at the Coliseum.[70] William Wilson recalled the summer of 1925:

> *I stood one steaming August noonday at the corner of Seventh and Main and watched them march past, men on horseback, men in cars, men on foot, women, children, all in robes, all hooded, some carrying naming [sic] crosses on long poles, silent except for the hum of motors and the clop of hooves and the soft shuffle of shoes on the half-molten asphalt. Afterward, the newspapers said there were more than five thousand of them....I wondered how many of them were our neighbors on Chandler Avenue.*[71]

In November, thousands came to the Coliseum to hear Joe Huffington speak—according to the *Journal* it was "jammed to the roof and the crowd on the outside stood...for two hours to hear the address relayed to them by a microphone and loud speakers." He promised the crowd, "If the people of Evansville will join hands with the Klan, we will see to it that there is good government."[72] As Dana Caldemeyer argued, by emphasizing concerns about law enforcement, corruption and immigration, the Klan was able to establish itself in Evansville in the mid-1920s. By 1927–28, however, its power was gone, destroyed by infighting, corruption and Stephenson's violent criminality; in James Madison's memorable words, "Behind the screen of the Klan's machine were corrupt windbags and bungling fools, squabbling among themselves for money and power."[73]

Despite the very real presence of deep racism, crushing poverty and the grotesquery of the Klan, overall the first three decades of the twentieth century were economically good for Evansville, and this period is marked by a remarkable list of buildings and institutions that are with us still. The YMCA (1914), the McCurdy Hotel (1917), the Soldiers and Sailors Memorial Coliseum (1917) and Bosse Field (1915) all went up then, along with Evansville College's Administration Hall (1922) and four high schools: FJ Reitz (1918), Benjamin Bosse (1924), Reitz Memorial (1925) and Lincoln (1928). Lincoln High School was exclusively for Black students and, despite its name, included elementary classes too; the last high school class graduated in 1962, when it became, as it continues today, a K–8 school. Bosse Field is lauded as "the third oldest ballpark in the country used for professional baseball on a regular basis, surpassed only by Fenway Park [1912] in Boston and Wrigley Field [1914] in Chicago."[74] Some spectacular bank buildings that still stand were erected at this time,

Evansville College's Administration Hall under construction, circa 1922. *IGWS/IU.*

including the American Trust and Savings (1904) at Sixth and Main, City National (1913) at Third and Main and Citizens National (1916) at Fourth and Main.[75] The latter was said to be the first skyscraper in the city, and according to the *Courier*, "A great white shaft, 163 feet tall, has obtruded itself on the Evansville skyline during 1915 and in appearance is easily the most striking new building erected in twenty years."[76] Arguably an even more striking new building arrived on the downtown scene in September 1930 when the ten-story art deco Central Union Bank was opened at Fourth and Sycamore. Called "a Monument to the Spirit of Enterprise," it was described as "a beautiful jewel" whose "towering form of ten stories of beautiful limestone fashioned after the modernistic motif is a landmark which transforms the neighborhood."[77] This magnificent building has graced downtown ever since, but it has been severely neglected and in the summer of 2022 was placed on Indiana Landmarks' "10 Most Endangered List." Of all the buildings in Evansville from this era, it is clearly the most at risk of being lost.[78] It was not just physical structures that were being built at this time—contemporaneously several businesses that were going to become parts of the fabric of the city established themselves. These included Hercules Buggy, Fendrich Cigar, George Koch Sons, Hoosier

Benjamin Bosse. *EVPL.*

Lamp and Stamping, Bucyrus Steam Shovel, Bernardin Bottle Cap, Graham Glass, Faultless Caster and Mead Johnson.[79]

This was also the era of Benjamin Bosse (1875–1922), one of the most influential men in Evansville's history. The son of German immigrants, Bosse was a successful businessman with widespread interests including furniture, banking, insurance, realty, coal, hotels and the *Evansville Courier*, which he owned from December 1920. He served as the city's mayor from 1914 until his sudden death in 1922, aged forty-seven.

His impact on the city was gigantic, and people from all walks of life and all eras have sung his praises, up to and including the last four mayors of Evansville. The sesquicentennial history of the city summed Bosse up:

> *He challenged sleepy businessmen to get something done, banged on tables, gathered support from everybody and remodeled the fire department, built the police station, organized the city recreation department and prodded both the school people and the citizens to get more and better schools. He was the driving force behind both Garvin and Mesker Parks.*[80]

He is remembered for the slogan "When everybody boosts, everybody wins," which was first publicly unveiled at the opening of Bosse Field in 1915,[81] and his impressive legacy also includes the University of Evansville (UoE), better transport infrastructure, Bosse Field itself, housing codes, the Coliseum, the Market and city swimming pools. In the words of the most recent holder of the office, Lloyd Winnecke, "Without a doubt, Mayor Benjamin Bosse was one of our city's greatest leaders. His style and enthusiasm for Evansville may never be matched. His vision and philanthropy, in addition to his leadership, are the standards by which all of his successors will be judged."[82] It should also be said, among all this praise, that Bosse was a politician at a time of some deeply corrupt politics and a businessman at a time of some deeply corrupt business practices. The historian Dana Caldemeyer said of Bosse, "During his eight years as Evansville mayor Bosse ran the city with a firm fist and turned a blind eye to corruption. He ensured that the city purchased coal from his Bosse Coal Company, bribed voters, and hired his friends rather than the lowest bidder to perform maintenance on city roads and buildings."[83] Even his own most recent biographer conceded that vote buying and election fraud were endemic in the city at that time but pointed out that "Benjamin Bosse was never indicted for anything…[although] that may seem like a very low bar."[84]

As Bosse took office in 1914, the events taking place in Europe that summer were largely ignored in Evansville, but their impact was to be felt soon enough. As one diplomatic crisis rolled into another, the major powers of Europe plunged rapidly into the most destructive global conflict in human history. Germany was at the heart of it, and Evansville was a city with substantial German cultural influences. Benjamin Bosse was raised and schooled as a German speaker and up to 1914 attended churches whose worship was entirely in German.[85] In the words of the educator Louis Bénézet, "Plenty of our people were pro-German and understandably so, as late as January 1917."[86] By 1917, however, the United States had entered the war as an enemy of Germany, with profound effects on the German culture of Evansville.[87] As the labor historian Samuel White said, "All German-language newspapers ceased publication, churches stopped offering German-language services, and the schools removed the German language from their curriculums."[88] Inevitably, much of the city's German culture was lost as a result of that process. While there are still some German cultural expressions, especially on the West Side of Evansville, the deep and authentic German culture is mostly gone.

Whatever their family background, many local people joined the war effort, and it is estimated that around 4,000 men and women from Evansville and Vanderburgh County served. The Evansville chapter of the Red Cross was extremely active during the war, making and shipping over 300,000 surgical dressings and almost 16,000 knitted garments, among thousands of other items.[89] In a remarkable example of lost history that has been painstakingly recovered, the Vanderburgh County Clerk's Archive contains recently discovered records that reveal that as many as 150 local women served as military nurses during the war. This was a section of World War 1 history that had all but disappeared until the dedicated work of Amber Gowen, the county clerk's archivist.[90] Approximately 85 local men died in the war, a mix of those killed by enemy action and those who died from illness, mostly the Spanish flu. Noteworthy among the lost were two brothers, Paul and Albert Funkhouser; Paul was killed in action in the Argonne, France, in October 1918, and Albert, who developed pneumonia as a result of having been gassed, died in Virginia in 1919.[91]

In an interesting echo of the fact that Evansville's John Smith Gavitt was claimed to be the first Indiana officer to be killed in the Civil War,[92]

The funeral of James Bethel Gresham at Locust Hill Cemetery, 1921. *USI.*

James Bethel Gresham of Evansville was one of the first three American soldiers to be killed in action in World War I.[93] He was killed in hand-to-hand fighting near Bathelémont, France, on November 3, 1917. Initially buried in France, with a monument over the grave site, Gresham was returned to the United States and buried in Evansville's Locust Hill cemetery in July 1921. Gresham is most definitely not "lost history"—his death was widely recognized at the time and has remained in the public eye ever since. The city raised money to buy his widowed mother a home on the edge of Garvin Park in 1918, and there is a flag and marker on the hill above his grave. He is also commemorated prominently at the Indiana War Memorial complex in Indianapolis, where the cenotaph is dedicated to his memory, and like the Funkhouser brothers, there is a veterans organization in Evansville that bears his name. In 2017, on the centenary of Gresham's death, the French consul-general in Chicago, Guillaume Lacroix, came down to Evansville to lay a wreath on his grave.[94]

The interwar years were tumultuous in Evansville and left their mark on the city in numerous ways. Some of these marks are more visible today than others, and some have been lost entirely. It was a period when

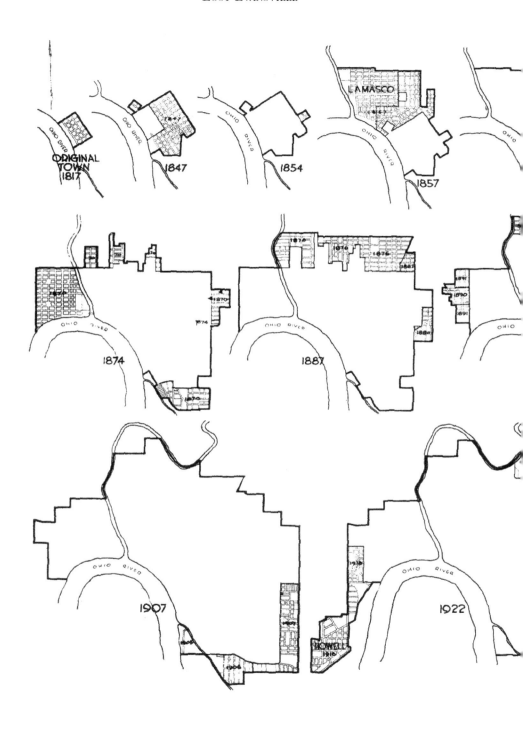

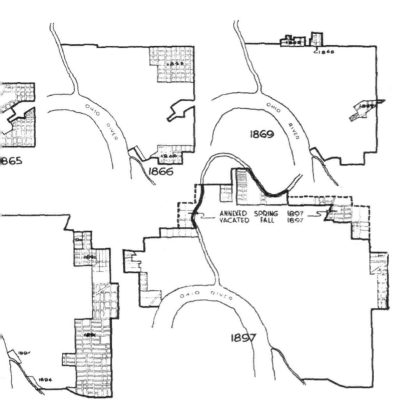

THE GROWTH
OF
EVANSVILLE
INDIANA

THE FIGURE UNDER EACH STAGE
OF GROWTH REFERS TO THE
BOUNDARY OF THAT PARTICULAR
YEAR— SHOWN BY A H E A V Y
OUTLINE.
PLATTED PORTIONS ARE AN-
NEXATIONS, THE YEAR OF
EACH BEING INDICATED.

CITY PLAN COMMISSION
HARLAND BARTHOLOMEW - CITY PLAN ENGINEER
SAINT LOUIS · MISSOURI

The expansion
of the city up to
1926. *EVPL*

Evansville became a major player in the automobile market, with three key companies leading the way. In the 1920s, the Graham Brothers, using Dodge engines, became the biggest exclusive truck builder in the world—in 1926 they sold 37,463 units and in 1927 over 56,000 trucks worldwide.[95] "When we were boys and young men," recalled an elderly Joseph Graham in 1988 with impressive hyperbole, "Evansville was the capital of the universe."[96] The Hercules Buggy company was established by William H. McCurdy in 1902, and shortly after they began to build bodies that could be combined with engines in Chicago to form the Sears Motor Buggy. Other relationships followed, including with the Ford Motor company, and the company—with various offshoots—flourished at their sprawling facilities centered on Morton Avenue. In 1922 Hercules produced over 80,000 carriages and buggies, over 60,000 gas engines and some 40,000 auto and truck bodies.[97] The company eventually moved into refrigeration and in 1925 became Servel, a company that would dominate Evansville for decades. The third and final major player in the local automotive industry was Chrysler, which began manufacturing in Evansville in 1935. They operated in cooperation with Briggs Manufacturing and primarily built Plymouth cars, the company's remarkably successful entry into the lower-priced market.[98] The appeal of Evansville was—as so often in the past—the proximity of the Ohio River, and most of these Plymouths were shipped out through the Mead Johnson Terminal, a $500,000 state-of-the-art rail-truck-river terminal that originally opened in February 1931. For decades, its marketing slogan was "Where waterway, railway, highway meet."[99] "With the completion of the terminal," trumpeted the *Courier* in a front-page splash, "Evansville takes its place in the river transportation world along with Pittsburgh, Cincinnati, Louisville, St Louis and Memphis as an inland port of consequence, river men say….Evansville is now the best equipped inland city in the United States for river-rail transfer and storage."[100] Chrysler had built and shipped out 1 million cars by March 1953, and by the end of their Evansville tenure they had produced over 1.7 million Plymouths.[101] Today, there is virtually no sign of all this success, although many of the factory buildings still remain. The battered and fading gray roof of the Mead Johnson Terminal shed sticking out over the river and the word *Hercules* on an old foundry building that faces the main east–west expressway in the city are about the sum of it, and even these surely go unnoticed by the vast majority. In October 2022, a massive fire destroyed much of what had been the Hercules Buggy and Servel facilities around Morton Avenue. Truly, a lost history.

Hercules Buggy Co., Evansville, Ind.   Largest Vehicle Factory in the World.
Capital Stock $1,000,000.00.

The sprawling Hercules Buggy facility, later Servel. *EVPL.*

"There were many, many companies," recalled William B. Koch in 2016, "[that] just went belly-up, and people were looking for work." He was speaking of the Great Depression, which profoundly affected Evansville, as it did every other city in the country. Although largely unmarked and perhaps little remembered, some of the vestiges of that time do remain in the city today. Local industries were hit hard almost immediately, as was farming. "I remember that people were at the back door every day, begging for food," said Claude "J" Wertz. "They were just people wandering the streets who were hungry, and they'd say, 'Lady, can you give me a sandwich?' They were there almost every day." Koch's family lived on North Third Avenue close to a railroad, and he remembered, "We would have 'hoboes' come around, and Mom would give them a sandwich."[102] Eight local banks shut down inside three months in 1931–32, starting with the Lincoln Bank on October 4, 1931, and climaxing on January 12, 1932, when, in what James Morlock called "another outbreak of hysteria," three banks closed in one day—Franklin Trust and Savings, the Howell Bank and the West Side Bank, which had been founded by Benjamin Bosse in 1903.[103] The Central Union Bank in its magnificent new art deco skyscraper—which had opened just sixteen months before—closed on January 11. Its life as a bank had lasted only one month more than it had taken to build.[104]

Supplement celebrating the opening of Central Union Bank, 1930. *EVPL.*

Unemployment rose to eleven thousand—a rate of 25 percent; in comparison, by far the highest rate that has been seen in the past thirty-two years was 15.1 percent in April 2020 at the height of the COVID-19 pandemic.[105] Robert Hartman, growing up on West Virginia Street, recalled "his family's shotgun-style house with no insulation and the ill-fitting clothes his mother fashioned from old jackets and coveralls and the corncobs that were mixed with coal in the furnace to save money."[106] Shirley Stucki, living in Evansville with her grandparents, said, "I remember standing in line at the Coliseum around Christmas with a lot of other poor kids. Some civic groups pitched in and every child could get one gift. My choice came down to a red-handled broom or a doll. I took the broom because there was always a mess under the coal stove, and I wanted to do my part by keeping that part of the house clean."[107] Shanty towns sprang up, one between St. Joseph Avenue and Wabash Avenue, another at Seventh Avenue and Pennsylvania and a third along Pigeon Creek. "Most of the locations," said the *Press* in 1937, "have a decided odor."[108] One of the shanties made a lifelong impression on young Robert Hartman:

> *The first time I really saw poverty in Evansville was when I went to shantytown along the river with my father, Adolph….I was maybe 9 years old, and he told me to tag along….The houses, if that's what you want to call them, had roofs made from pop and beer signs. There was no plumbing. The walls were made of whatever they could find. There weren't any beds, just mattresses. Many of the people wore free county-issue footwear which you could easily tell by the black high-top shoes and the black socks that rode up over the knee. Walking up the plank to get to one of those places is something I'll never forget.*[109]

Desperate times produced a remarkable response, however, and millions of dollars of New Deal government money helped stabilize the banking and financial sector. In addition, by the mid-1930s several of the New Deal's "alphabet soup agencies" were active in Evansville, with many of the projects being worked on or funded through more than one of these agencies. The Civilian Conservation Corps (CCC) set up a camp at St. Joseph Avenue and Buchanan Road, and workers upgraded and developed hundreds of acres of Mesker Park; there are parts of the existing zoo that are a product of this work. The New Deal, like almost everything else in American life, was discriminatory, but it "at least included blacks within the pool of beneficiaries" and some of these CCC workers in Evansville were Black.[110] The Civil Works Administration (CWA) organized minor jobs around town, the Workers' Service Program (WSP) planned various educational projects,[111] while the Works Progress Administration (WPA) was responsible for building and repairing roads, installing sidewalks,

A Black WPA crew resurfacing Wabash Avenue, 1936. *USI.*

building sewers, paving streets and constructing city and county garages. They helped expand and renovate Burdette Park, a city park named for another local man killed in World War I that still brings joy to countless people year-round. They also removed the now-obsolete streetcar tracks that still ran down Main Street. Vitally for the preservation of the city's distant past, a WPA crew of 277 excavated Angel Mounds between 1937 and 1942, uncovering almost 2.4 million objects; material and data from these digs are still being used by academic archaeologists today. The site's most celebrated artifact, a small figurine of a kneeling man, was uncovered by the WPA workers.[112] Women WPA workers restored and reformed the binding of over 200,000 books for the Central and Willard Libraries. The WPA's Historical Records Survey worked to produce an index of all public county records from 1818 to 1940, making a gigantic contribution to the preservation of the area's history. According to the current county clerk's archivist, "The inventories remain a pivotal reference in understanding the documents created and held by county government agencies. Without the foundation provided by the records survey, many vital local government documents, as well as their historical context, would be lost."[113] There was a WPA Band that played concerts from 1936 to 1942, broadcast their music on local radio station WGBF and performed before basketball games. "Harry High, director," said the *Press* in 1936, "has formed a splendid dance orchestra, German band, and jug band from the organization."[114] Further significant contributions came from the Public Works Administration (PWA), whose money funded and whose members worked on Washington Elementary School, the new National Guard armory on Rotherwood Avenue, two Pigeon Creek bridges, the first Dress Plaza flood barrier and the Lincoln Gardens Black public housing project.[115] Overall, it was an enormous multifaceted set of initiatives from 1933 to 1942 that prevented the city from going under. Evansville was literally saved from disaster by New Deal money and federal programs, without which much more than jobs would have been lost. In early 1937, however, a different kind of disaster loomed.

In 1926, the *Courier*'s cartoonist Karl Kae Knecht drew a cartoon that depicted the Ohio River as "Our Giant"—a gigantic working elephant several times bigger than life size. The picture is a metaphor for the huge positive potential of the river, but the potential for chaos is present too—a tiny human figure guides the giant with an even tinier elephant hook, and he looks like he is straining to do so. At any moment, the pacified giant might break free. In January 1937 it did just that, with the most severe river flood in U.S. history, overwhelming houses, workplaces and farms and driving one million midwesterners from their homes. Hundreds died, and it did hundreds of millions of dollars in damage.[116] Journalist Rich Davis called it

WPA men conducting the archaeological dig at Angel Mounds, 1940. *IUMAA.*

Evansville underwater, 1937. *USI.*

"the greatest natural disaster in the history of Evansville"; the Ohio rose a horrifying nineteen feet above its flood stage here, inundating five hundred city blocks, damaging thousands of homes and completely destroying many buildings close to the river.[117] The transformation of the river from servant to monster was elegantly summarized in a local publication two months later: "The river which has been a source of the valley's greatness, which has provided avenues of commerce, watered our richest farmlands, and added to the scenic loveliness of our region, became almost overnight the mightiest and most fearsome enemy our people have ever had to face."[118] With a gargantuan response from federal, state and local organizations including the National Guard, the Red Cross and the WPA, the city managed to prevent any loss of life and was able to maintain an adequate level of services to the population. One of the heroes of the hour was Paul H. Schmidt, then president of the Evansville chapter of the Red Cross. Schmidt realized early that the flood was coming and started organizing the city's response a full two weeks before the flood hit; he was therefore probably responsible for the lack of flood deaths in the city.[119] From the perspective of preventing the loss of history, Schmidt is, if anything, an even bigger hero. In addition to everything else that he organized in the frenetic days leading up to and during the flood, Schmidt also set up an Archive Commission "to write a record of the tragedy which visited our community so that it would be available for the living and for generations to come." The 1977 printed edition of the commission's work spells out their impact:

> *If it were not for the on-the-scene accounts written by members of the Archive Commission, in a few more decades the story of the disaster would be largely forgotten and a brilliant period in Evansville's history lost. But because Paul H. Schmidt…had a sense of history and of the need to preserve accounts of the event for future generations, a knowledge of those dramatic happenings can now be in the possession of anyone interested.*[120]

For that and many other reasons, the city is in Schmidt's debt.

Having weathered the storm both literally and figuratively, Evansville's people looked forward to the 1940s with optimism. Events in Europe and Asia, however, were going to affect that outlook in ways that no one could have imagined.

2

The men at the meeting were worried. They had good reason to be. The group that gathered at lunchtime on July 1, 1941, at the Lamplight Inn on Second Street at the invitation of the Central Labor Union was remarkably diverse: Democratic mayor William Dress; Louis Ruthenburg, president of Servel; Bert Martin, president of the Central Labor Union; F.B. Culley, president of the chamber of commerce; and C.B. Enlow, president of National City Bank. The huge concern that served to unify this disparate group was that Evansville was going to become a ghost town as the country moved onto a war footing and nonessential manufacturing became sidelined. As a city with only a couple of plants working on military contracts, Evansville was not positioned to benefit from a potential war economy; Arthur Eberlin of the chamber of commerce called Evansville "the forgotten country" when it came to military contracts.[121] Mayor Dress observed at the meeting, "Operations of firms engaged only in production of peace-time goods are bound to decline as war goods production is stepped up. Unless we have defense industries to absorb the workers, the situation might become acute." He expressed optimism, however, "if everybody works together." Bert Martin added, "Evansville, with its advantages as to location, transportation, labor supply and other facilities, we believe, should be utilized for defense production. This cannot happen unless we can locate defense industries here or unless our established manufacturers obtain defense contracts."[122] It was a big ask, but almost incredibly, that was exactly what happened.

LSTs under construction at the Evansville Shipyard; Reitz High School top right. Image was restricted until after the war. *EVPL.*

Labor leaders used their national union connections; politicians called in favors and used their relationships, all the way up to the Oval Office; and businessmen used their nationwide networks. The synergy this produced was to transform the city.[123]

The transformation began almost immediately, with orders being signed as early as January 1942, and by spring, two huge new industrial projects had been announced, each unlike anything Evansville had seen before. In February, the press revealed that a navy shipyard would be built on forty-five derelict acres on the Ohio River beside the Mead Johnson Terminal at which an "unlimited number of 300-foot boats will be constructed," and a month later, news broke that "construction is expected to begin immediately on a new airplane assembly plant to be built here by the Republic Aviation Corporation."[124] The shipyard, employing 19,200 workers at its peak, would eventually build 167 Landing Ship Tanks (LSTs) that were among the single most important pieces of technology produced during the war. It is difficult to imagine how a war that included so many crucial amphibious assaults on fortified beaches could have succeeded without the Allies having the ability to land large numbers of tanks and other heavy equipment directly onto beaches. In 1944 alone, the yard produced 95 ships, at an approximate rate of one ship every four days.[125] Republic Aviation, with a peak workforce of 8,300, built the highly versatile P-47 Thunderbolt, a plane that saw action all over Europe and the Pacific as a fighter, an escort, a ground-attack aircraft and a ship-buster. Within twenty months of breaking ground for construction of the plant, they had built and delivered 1,000 aircraft, and over the course of its life the factory averaged 14 P-47s per day for a total of 6,670 Thunderbolts. Nowhere else in the world produced both LSTs and P-47s, and had Evansville done nothing else, the city's contribution to Allied victory would have been immense. But it did a lot more.

Despite the importance of the shipyard and of Republic, most Evansville war work was carried on at other plants that were already here, and it is estimated that forty-eight local companies were involved. The industrial population shot up from approximately 18,000 before the war to over 80,000 at its wartime peak. The Evansville Chrysler factory on Maxwell Avenue became the Evansville Ordnance plant, and workers test-fired the first .45-caliber bullets off the production line a mere ninety days after conversion from car production had begun. They produced more .45 bullets in one day than the whole prewar U.S. small arms industry produced in a year, and they ultimately produced billions of rounds of ammunition and reconditioned

The Evansville Ordnance plant in the Chrysler factory (*center left*), with the purpose-built bullet-loading facility in the foreground. *USI.*

thousands of tanks and trucks.[126] Their workforce ballooned from 650 in 1941 to 12,560 by the fall of 1943.[127] Servel, which by now occupied all the factory space once held by Hercules, switched from making refrigerators to producing many different war-related items, including thousands of pairs of wings for P-47s, landmines, engine parts and millions of shell casings. They also built field ranges, airplane head castings and landing gear assemblies. Their workforce was 15,000 in 1943. International Steel made hull sections for the LSTs, pontoon combat bridges and Bailey portable bridges. Briggs, employing 6,000 people in 1943, produced wings for the U.S. Navy's Corsair aircraft. Hoosier Cardinal manufactured P-47 tail assemblies, bomb racks and plastic bomber domes, while Sunbeam Electric made many items, including rocket nozzles and rifle grenades.[128] Faultless Caster was the country's biggest manufacturer of casters—an often-ignored but vital cog in the American production behemoth that eventually was able to crush the Axis.[129] In the end, fourteen Evansville plants won the coveted Army-Navy "E" Award, with nine of them winning it multiple times.[130] It was a truly remarkable effort from a city that, had it not been for its own proactive exertions, might well have ended up with none of it.

The Second World War was simultaneously Evansville's greatest challenge and its greatest triumph. Thousands of Evansville men and women served in uniform, and hundreds of men were killed; their names are recorded on often-neglected war memorials across town.[131] Against long odds, the city secured multiple war orders and was then able to provide the skilled labor needed to fulfill them all. One key to this was the maintenance of functioning relations between labor and management, despite ongoing conflict. Evansville had a long and bitter history of struggle between union organizers and management and owners who deplored unions. The fight to unionize did not stop during the war, but for the most part it did not get in the way of production, although there were exceptions. Ruthenburg at Servel, along with the management at Bucyrus-Erie and Seeger, "led a concerted effort by large industrial employers in Evansville to hold off unionization during the Second World War." In the end, however, at least in the short term, the unions were to win this fight. By 1946, the United Electrical, Radio and Machine Workers of America (UE) were able to organize at Servel and at least five other large companies until their Local 813 was the largest union in the city with around seven thousand members.[132] Another key to the city's ability to supply workers was its successful deployment of migrant workers from surrounding areas, women and Black people. Despite many problems, injustices and inequities, the city managed to keep the materials

The Republic Aviation plant. *EVPL.*

flowing.[133] And the story is not just about the supply of labor but involves all the massively complex logistics of wartime production: a working transport infrastructure; on-time supplies of raw materials; the constantly changing array of machinery, tools and dies; accommodation for tens of thousands of incomers in subdivided private homes, trailer parks, newly built apartments and six sprawling federal housing projects; schools for their children and

Industrial Evansville's heart during World War II: from bottom, Evansville Ordnance (Chrysler), Faultless Caster, Briggs and Servel. *USI.*

transport to get them there; the provision of food and drink; entertainment for nonworking hours; and a host of other difficult issues. All that was done in Evansville was done well enough, enough of the time, to get the job done. And because of this remarkable effort—in Evansville and in thousands of other cities across the free world—the Allies won the war. Because in the end, the reason the Allies won the war was the sheer massive scale of American production, which was able eventually to swamp the Axis on multiple fronts simultaneously. As the historian David Kennedy has pointed out, "Every American combatant in the last year and a half of war in the Pacific islands could draw on four tons of supplies; his Japanese opponent, just two pounds."[134] One need only glance at photos of Evansville-built LSTs disgorging Allied forces and supplies onto beaches across Europe and the Pacific to realize that this city's efforts from 1942 to 1945 more than played a part in changing the world.[135]

And then, finally and rather suddenly, it was all over. A gigantic global war that began in China in 1937 and started for Americans on December 7, 1941, concluded on August 14, 1945. Evansville immediately exploded into a huge street party, with thousands of people jamming Main Street in "a victory binge that lasted far, far into the night."[136] "There was nothing but joy," said Judge Holbrook, a Black man who worked at Briggs. "Some of the people were so elated and so overjoyed that they just stopped working at that particular moment and told their supervisors they wanted to get out and celebrate." "Downtown was bedlam," added Servel worker John Payne. "Everybody was uproariously happy….No one knew what they were saying. I thought it would never end. It went on for hours and hours and hours."[137]

The party did end, however, and so did Evansville's war production. The war economy in the city had always been a complicated and variable phenomenon—one of the characteristics of Evansville war plants had been their remarkable ability to pivot from the production of one item to another. Chrysler had gone from cars to brass bullets, to steel bullets, to refitting tanks, to refitting trucks, to finally working on a contract to make a staggering 7.6 million incendiary cluster bombs.[138] The shipyard launched its last LST in February 1945, then switched to making other kinds of vessels, and by the summer of 1945 a large group of its personnel were literally on ships sailing to Pearl Harbor to help set up a repair facility there. Servel pivoted multiple times from the production of one item to another, making twenty-six different products, while Hoosier Cardinal did the same as it produced twenty-three separate items for the war effort.[139] In mid-August, Servel and Hoosier Cardinal were already pivoting again, preparing for peacetime production even before the war ended—what the *Press* called "juggling their operations to reduce their reconversion period to a minimum." Servel boss Louis Ruthenburg sent a memo to his middle managers at that time, saying, "In all likelihood cancellation of war contracts will take place more abruptly than we anticipated."[140]

The morning after the huge Evansville street party the night before, workers awoke not just with sore heads but with news that five of the biggest war plants would be affected by the immediate cancellation of three of their biggest orders.[141] Harold Morgan's father worked at Republic Aviation, and Morgan recalled in 2016, "Dad was terminated the day after Japan surrendered." "All these factories that were making war goods," said historian Jon Carl, "quit making war goods. Literally overnight. They stopped the orders and they quit making airplanes, and ships, and bullets."[142] Within a day, 10,650 workers were estimated to have lost their jobs at local war plants. The Chrysler cluster bomb order was canceled, and the phosphorus that would have gone into the bombs was transported up to the powder farm on Highway 41 and burned.[143] On September 5, 1945, the already reduced workforce of 1,700 at the shipyard learned that the last order was canceled, and twenty days later the navy announced that the yard was surplus property; orders were canceled even for ships that were already more than half-built. The men who were sailing to Pearl Harbor were turned around and sent back home.[144]

Things might have looked grim at that moment, but instead, the local economy surged.[145] As Jon Carl put it, "Because all of these workers had been making more money than they had ever made and not being able to spend it because there weren't consumer goods to buy, everybody had a down payment for a new house, and everybody had a down payment for a new car."[146] There were also many households with two or more earners for the first time, and according to one observer, Rolland Eckels, "When the war was over, there was a tremendous amount of money available."[147] Local plants managed to pivot to postwar life extremely quickly, hoping to take advantage of the 1.8 million square feet increase in available space.[148] In mid-August, it was said that Servel expected to begin production of

Evansville in 1946. *USI.*

refrigerators by October 15; Seeger-Sunbeam planned to start work on refrigerators by September 1; and Bucyrus-Erie planned to continue their output of tractors and bulldozers.[149]

Evansville's ability to pivot quickly to a postwar reality was no accident; in fact, it was the product of intensive planning that had gone on for over three years. As early as May 1942, Louis Ruthenburg was speaking of "the great new world which lies beyond the present scene of armed conflict…a new world which must be different to the one in which we have lived."[150] He was on the board of trustees and Indiana chairman of the Committee for Economic Development (CED), a national business group established by the Department of Commerce in September 1942 whose stated purpose was "to see to it that the economy did not collapse when the war effort was over and the war contracts were cancelled." Prominent local business leaders Thomas J. Morton and Walter Koch were also active members.[151] Clearly, local politicians were also considering the issues, and Mayor Manson Reichert talked about a somewhat nebulous "program of post-war construction and improvement projects to take up slack in employment at the close of the war" in March 1943,[152] but things became more organized with the establishment of Evansville's Postwar Planning Council (EPPC) the following month. It was born at a meeting in the McCurdy Hotel, and F.B. Culley, president of the chamber of commerce, was picked to head the group. The range of their interests, and the scale of the task that they faced, is reflected by the fact that they immediately organized ten committees that were tasked with reporting back within thirty days with "suggestions" on topics that ranged from industry and agriculture to transportation, education, labor and civilian defense.[153]

The discussion continued when the CED held a conference in Evansville in December 1943 at which local business leaders were urged to prepare with urgency for the postwar situation. Ruthenburg warned ominously, "There'll be no tapering off of war contracts. Yours will end like a bolt from the blue."[154] Showing an impressive level of community involvement at all levels, the EPPC asked the West Side Nut Club in February 1944 to conduct "a survey of proposed post-war improvements and job needs on the West Side," and in May, Culley attended a statewide postwar planning conference that was organized by Indiana governor Henry F. Schricker.[155] The labor unions were also planning for the future, and in July 1944, Julius Emspak, one of the most prominent national leaders of the UE, told a postwar planning conference in Evansville, "We don't want to go back to the apple-selling days which followed World War One because no plans were made for the war's end.…If we can convert our plants to manufacture munitions for destruction, we can reconvert them to provide jobs."[156]

In January 1945, Culley delivered the first complete public report on the EPPC's work and, interestingly for a group that was dominated by conservative businessmen, he stressed the importance of labor and celebrated past achievements, saying, "Evansville has operated during the war period without strikes. This is a distinct contribution by this war production city and an evidence of the intelligence and fairmindedness of both labor and management."[157] The same month, Gilmore Haynie, director of the War Production Board (WPB) in Evansville, sent a report to John Nuveen, who was WPB chief in Chicago, asking for government help with the postwar situation in Evansville. With so many cooks in the kitchen, in April, a three-man committee was assembled whose task was, according to the *Press*: the "conversion of a jumble of major postwar plans into a systematic, long-range program.…A master plan [which] will list the proposed projects according to need and availability of funds."[158] By July, the EPPC decided that the task was too big and complex for amateurs and the city and county governments agreed to find almost $13,000 to pay for the work of "master planner" Earl O. Mills of St Louis.[159]

As the postwar economy thrived, production was concentrated in a small number of large companies, and by 1953, Evansville's "Big Four"—Servel, International Harvester, Seeger-Sunbeam and Chrysler—employed 63 percent of the manufacturing workforce. The first three of these companies were mostly focused on the manufacture of refrigerators, leading to the city's oft-repeated claim to be the "refrigerator capital of the world."[160] Servel had been in the business of refrigerators for a long time, commanding around 6 percent of the market in 1933 and producing over 1 million gas refrigerators by 1937, while Sunbeam had been making the "Coldspot" refrigerator for Sears since the 1920s and merged with Seeger in 1945.[161] International Harvester had been in Evansville since the early 1900s but made the move into domestic appliances at the end of the war and purchased the Republic Aviation plant from the government in January 1946 for $5.65 million. This purchase was partly facilitated by an Evansville committee that traveled to Washington, DC, three months before to stress the importance of getting the plant sold to a viable business.[162] Chrysler went back to making cars, producing Plymouths at a remarkable rate—400 per day on average and 800 per day in December 1954. At one time when demand was particularly high, Plymouths moved off the line at the rate of 100 per hour.[163] Thirty thousand Evansville

Several hundred Chrysler-made Plymouths await being loaded onto barges in 1959. The parking lot is the former site of the Evansville Shipyard. *EVPL.*

citizens attended an open house at the plant to celebrate the millionth car rolling off the production line in March 1953, and by the time the plant closed in 1959, they had produced 1,701,163 Plymouths.[164]

Additional stimulus to many Evansville industries was provided by the Korean War from 1950 to 1953, when local industry became war industry for the second time in a decade. As with every war, there was also a high price to pay in blood—in only three years, over 36,500 Americans died in Korea. Many local men were killed or injured, including members of C Company, Sixteenth Infantry Battalion, the local U.S. Marine Corps Reserve unit, whose young men were sent to fight despite being almost untrained and wholly unprepared.[165] But at home there was lots of money to be made. Chrysler built hulls for the Grumman Albatross, a flying boat used for patrolling and search and rescue. International Steel produced Bailey Bridges and railroad car parts; Seeger made tail parts and fuselage sections for the F-86 Sabrejet; Servel and Hoosier Cardinal worked on Republic F-84 Thunderjet and F-84F Thunderstreak airplane wings and Servel also made steel cartridge cases for 105mm recoilless rifles; International Harvester produced $32 million worth of rifles; clothing companies went into uniform production; Bucyrus-Erie found a majority of its output purchased for the war effort; Bootz made practice bombs; Keller-Crescent printed Air Force manuals; George Mesker made steel for the Atomic Energy Commission; and at Faultless Caster over one-third of their facilities were devoted to defense production by December

1951.[166] Servel had so much demand that they built a 121,000-square-foot facility on Virginia Street in 1951 to build the wings. Red Spot Paint and Varnish sold paint for defense industry facilities, General Tool and Die supplied equipment for defense plants around the country and even local food supply companies were involved in war production.[167] It was a multimillion-dollar windfall for the city, with a resultant massive effect on jobs; in March 1953, the employment number was 105,500, which was the highest monthly rate it would ever see between 1945 and 1970.

All seemed to be rosy, although there was clearly risk in a situation where, as Mau Tsai observed, "One out of every three wage and salary earners at that time was working for these four large firms."[168] In what can be seen as a symbolic demonstration of the vulnerability of the economy to sudden changes in circumstance, a devastating fire in January 1951 destroyed a large swathe of Main Street, costing millions of dollars and throwing hundreds out of work. After the end of the Korean War, that vulnerability proved more than symbolic. The mid- to late 1950s saw a series of major blows, as in a relatively short time period all four of the biggest local employers effectively disappeared. In the eloquent words of Kelley Coures,

> In 1956, Evansville was a humming engine of a city, growing and prosperous from VJ Day on. Proud and complacent, it was sure prosperity would last forever. Within a two-year period the city became a near ghost town as Servel, Chrysler and International Harvester packed up and moved out. The sudden rapture of its industrial base was its rude awakening.[169]

International Harvester and Seeger were both swallowed up by Whirlpool, Servel went out of business and Chrysler moved its production away to Fenton, Missouri. All four were facing some headwinds that were national or even international, and all had specific local issues too. There were three U.S. recessions in the decade after the Korean War: 1953–54, 1957–58 and 1960–61. Tastes and buying habits changed. As alternative transportation systems evolved, river transport began to seem slow and unreliable. Companies were moving away from old established factory sites in historic city centers in the Northeast and Midwest to purpose-built facilities in the South and West. Partly this was due to the invisible hand of market forces, but it was also driven by deliberate government policy—according to the historian Kenneth T. Jackson, federal tax laws encouraged "businesses to abandon old structures before their useful life is at an end by permitting greater tax benefits for new construction than for the improvement of

Evansville, 1949. Bottom right is Lincoln Gardens; the road moving diagonally across the image is Canal Street; top left is Briggs and below that is the sprawling campus of Servel. *USI.*

existing buildings." In effect, the government incentivized moving businesses to new locations.[170] Evansville, which had benefited enormously from federal largesse during the Great Depression and World War II, now had to watch as federal policies contributed to its decline.

As places like Evansville declined, other areas grew, and according to the geographer Luis Suarez-Villa, there was a rapid shift "of economic and political power away from the older industrial and metropolitan states of the Northeast and Midwest toward the Sunbelt."[171] One recent study, indeed, explained the rise of the sunbelt in terms that are particularly resonant to an Evansville audience: "The Northern productivity edge came from better access to waterways and a dense railroad network, advantages that became increasingly irrelevant as transportation costs plummeted during the 20th century."[172] Evansville's industry was therefore effectively swimming against a tide that made business as usual impossible. Chrysler, for example, moved away because the world of car-buying changed dramatically. It was elegantly summed up by journalist Ed Klingler in 1959:

Production became more complicated because of so many optional features offered to car buyers. Many dealers ordered most of their cars from the factory, practically custom built. The purchasers of these cars could not wait indefinitely for delivery by barge. So the river began to lose its importance to Chrysler. That meant Evansville also began to lose its importance to Chrysler.[173]

The last Evansville Chrysler car came off the assembly line on August 4, 1959.[174] In July 1955, after two months of swirling rumors, it was confirmed that Seeger was merging with the Whirlpool Corporation.[175] In September, the newly merged company purchased the International Harvester factory after that company made the decision to get out of a business in which it could no longer compete.[176]

Servel had put most of its eggs into the one basket of selling gas-powered ammonia absorption refrigerators while most of the market—up to 92 percent of it—was in electric compression refrigerators. It is a sobering reminder of Evansville's place in the refrigerator universe that the so-called refrigerator capital of the world does not get a single mention in a meticulously researched recent history of the industry. Servel, spending money trying to match the gigantic marketing power of its rivals, had also allowed its plants to become obsolete and inefficient and failed to make a profit in the years 1952–57.[177] In the end, one of the most significant companies in Evansville history was mostly sold off in parts. Its commercial refrigeration division was bought by Bendix-Westinghouse in 1956 to make compressors for air-conditioning units.[178] In September 1957, the Arkansas Louisiana Gas Company purchased the all-year air-conditioning division of Servel and set up a company called Arkla to run the business in Evansville.[179] And in January 1958, Whirlpool bought the Servel home appliance division, including all the patents, for $6.5 million.[180]

The combination of local factors and national trends led to some dark economic days in Evansville. Low-quality management-labor relations, poor local infrastructure and low morale have all been cited as contributory factors. When the city brought in an outside consulting firm—Fantus—in 1958, their much-cited two-volume final report was certainly scathing on the latter factor: "Evansville," said the Fantus Report, "is a city with a great inferiority complex....Evansville people feel that nothing can be done in Evansville.... Evansville is racked by pessimism, gloom [and the] inability to work in a unified fashion."[181] Some of roots for this might be seen a decade earlier, when national attention focused on the city's industrial and ideological fault lines. In the context of a rapidly worsening Cold War abroad, an expanding Red Scare at home and a coordinated nationwide campaign to "destroy the

Indiana state troopers at the Bucyrus-Erie plant, August 1948. *USI.*

militancy of the organized labor movement,"[182] several events in Evansville combined to make the city seem like an epicenter of instability.

In April, the third-party presidential candidate Henry Wallace— Roosevelt's vice president from 1941 to 1945 but widely smeared as a communist during this campaign—visited the city for a rally that was violently disrupted by anti-communist protesters, an event that was reported in the *New York Times*.[183] The Red Scare would eventually lead to over six hundred American college professors losing their jobs, but one of the first was George F. Parker of Evansville College, who was terminated within days of the rally for his public support of Wallace. The case aroused considerable national attention, and following a rigorous investigation, the college was censured by the Association of American University Professors, which spoke of "the damage done to the American tradition of freedom and to Evansville College, a damage which its Administration could have prevented had it possessed insight into the significance of intellectual freedom and courage to uphold those principles that are indispensable to the welfare of higher education and of the public."[184]

In the late summer of 1948, there was a bitter and at times violent strike at the Bucyrus-Erie plant; the strike was organized by UE Local 813, the city's largest and most active labor union. The union and its left-wing leadership had long been detested by the city's conservative business leaders, especially Louis Ruthenburg of Servel and H.R. Knox of Bucyrus-Erie. Ruthenburg was a forming member of the far-right anticommunist John Birch Society, and Knox in fact refused to negotiate with Local 813 on the grounds of his stated belief that it was communist-dominated. He could do this legally because under a recently passed amendment to the nation's labor laws, the Taft-Hartley Act of 1947, elected union officers had to affirm that they were not members of the Communist Party; the leaders of the UE had refused to do this.[185] There were violent confrontations at the picket lines, culminating on August 31 when 140 state troopers battled striking workers while the National Guard was on alert to intervene if required.[186] As a consequence of the strike, the Republican-led Congressional Labor and Education Committee held hearings in Evansville "to investigate Communist Influence in the Bucyrus-Erie Strike." Evansville's Republican congressman Edward Mitchell took a leading part in the hearings, asking each of the subpoenaed witnesses the question, "Are you now or have you ever been a member of the Communist Party?" He also repeatedly asked witnesses if they believed in God and if they were members of a church. Frustrated by the UE witnesses' refusal to answer many questions—they instead repeatedly read from a prepared statement—Mitchell angrily declared,

> *The people next door don't know what kind of termites they are living next door to, and I hope the press representatives will give them a good job of exposing these people who are putting on this three-ring circus, standing on their constitutional rights under the very Constitution that they are out to dishonor and overthrow by force and violence. We are not going to stop until we run them down.*[187]

His words were taken seriously by the local newspapers, which did indeed print the names and addresses of all the witnesses the next day.[188] Hostile witnesses named thirty-one people they claimed were communists (all subsequently named in the newspapers), and Representative Gerald Landis, who chaired the hearings, declared that the hearings "uncovered more evidence of communism in Evansville than had been expected." Local 813 responded by saying that "the people of Evansville have witnessed a sample of the kind of treatment that can be expected under the rule of those with a fascist ideology. The witch hunt just conducted was leveled at those who have actively fought the companies here in Evansville."[189] The "witch hunt" continued, as over the following days, many of those denounced were hounded out of their workplaces, and in the coming weeks dozens of workers at various plants were fired.[190]

But despite these events, and although there has been consistent messaging over the decades that the reason for the problems of the 1950s in Evansville was that the city was a "bad labor town," the reality was that labor-management relations were probably no worse than average. The left-leaning Local 813 was an exception, as most local unions did not share these sentiments, and there were fairly bitter rivalries between different unions. Evansville was an industrial city at a time of an intense nationwide struggle between organized labor and corporate management, which took place during a period of structural changes to the industrial economy. The *Courier* observed in a 1955 editorial that "the labor climate here is favorable for new industries....This is practical proof of the good relations between labor and management in Evansville....Evansville workers are responsible and loyal."[191] That comment was concurring with a public relations film called *Evansville Indiana, Balance Point, USA*, in which it was stated, "Labor, management, and civic officials pull together," and "Labor, and management know-how, and their willingness to work together in the spirit of friendly

Bendix-Westinghouse workers on strike, 1962. *USI.*

cooperation, are important foundation stones" of Evansville.[192] Indeed, L.L. Colbert, the national president of Chrysler, stated in 1957, "The labor situation in Evansville is no better nor a great deal worse" than in other cities where the company operated,[193] and even Louis Ruthenburg, sworn enemy of unions, believed that it was unfair that the city had such a reputation, saying, "Evansville has the best publicized strikes in the land."[194] Longtime local journalist Ed Klingler acknowledged the role of the newspapers: he said in a 1974 interview, "The newspapers have been accused of fomenting Evansville's labor reputation....I don't think any city in the United States covered their labor troubles in [the] excruciating detail that the Evansville papers did."[195]

Unemployment peaked in 1958 at 10.2 percent, a rate that would not be matched at any other point in the remainder of the century, and for the entire period of 1954–61, unemployment was never below 6.3 percent.[196] For comparison, even at the absolute height of the great recession that followed the financial crisis of 2007–8, local unemployment never reached 10 percent.[197] "Everyone cried doom," said one local historian, and "many

The giant Alcoa plant under construction, July 1957. *EVPL.*

predicted that Evansville was finished."[198] The city was by no means finished, however, and indeed the seeds of future success were being planted even during these dark days. Early energy was provided by the Evansville Council for Community Service, founded in 1946. Momentum continued with the Committee of 100, a business group that was formed in January 1952 to promote the city, and this was followed over the course of the 1950s by other groups such as the Committee for Evansville's Future Inc. and Evansville's Future. The Evansville Manufacturers and Employers Association Public Relations Division published a 190-page book in 1953 highlighting hundreds of different job types available in the city.[199] Various studies and reports were commissioned: two in 1954 and one each in 1956, 1957 and 1958.[200] While it seems that enough was learned from all that navel-gazing to ensure future successes, it needs to be stressed that a significant part of what happened to Evansville had almost nothing to do with the city itself—three nationwide recessions in eight years combined with tectonic shifts in the U.S. economy were going to rewire the local economy no matter what was done by the people of Evansville.

Relief was on its way. It started with aluminum production, with the *Courier* reporting in July 1956 that "work got underway on the gigantic task of cutting down hills and filling hollows and sloughs to make Alcoa's 6,000-acre tract north of Newburgh ready for construction of a 150,000-ton capacity smelter and power plant." After some delays, the power was eventually switched on in May 1960, and aluminum started to flow on June 10.[201] The plastics industry, a component of the Evansville economy since the 1930s, expanded enormously and by the 1970s was a significant player with such names as Ball, Sunbeam, Windsor and Crescent, among many more plastics companies that together employed thousands. In 1970, Ellis Carson, president of Sunbeam Plastics, could say, "The field is destined to grow, because more and more plastic products are being designed to replace similar metal and paper products, which are generally costlier," and by 1987, the area was being referred to as "Plastics Valley."[202] Much of that was in the future, but in fact, during the very time that Evansville's economy seemed bleakest, economist Mau Tsai estimated that a total of twenty-eight companies either "moved into the area or started local operations," and he termed the years 1962–69 a "period of recovery and self-improvement."[203] Much was lost from Evansville in this period, but the blows were far from fatal. In 1963, the governor of Indiana, Matthew Welsh, could declare in a speech at Roberts Stadium that "Evansville is now on the springboard of progress.…Evansville is the city that got its confidence back."[204] A major part of the springboard was infrastructure, to which we now turn.

3

T he thirty years after the end of World War II were undoubtedly
the single most significant era in Evansville's built history in terms
of shaping the city as it is in the third decade of the twenty-first
century. While obviously the basic parameters of the city are much
older—its location on the bend in the river, being split into east and west by
Pigeon Creek, the street grids that were first platted in the early nineteenth
century—much of the physical appearance of Evansville today is a direct
product of the changes to the built infrastructure that were made from
1946 to 1975. At times it seemed like Evansville thought about nothing
else—there were at least eight different sets of plans created between
the 1950s and the 1970s. Two major and expensive urban planning
exercises—by Victor Gruen in 1967 and Landeco Inc. in 1970—expended
thousands of words and painted beautiful pictures but had little lasting
impact on the city.[205] What actually happened, however, was in its own
way transformational. Although there was considerable overlap between
the different infrastructure initiatives, for the sake of clarity this chapter
divides these efforts into four separate parts: private and public housing,
alongside a discussion of the racism inherent in this process; urban renewal;
roadbuilding; and the construction of significant public buildings.

Firstly then, housing expanded with a significant increase of both public
and private housing, part of a nationwide process that the architectural
historian Barbara Miller Lane has called "houses for a new world."[206]
Although there were preexisting subdivisions in the city—including

Advertisement for a Guthrie May development, 1959. *EVPL.*

Iroquois Gardens under construction, 1947, looking east. At left is Division Street (now the Lloyd Expressway), crossing an undeveloped Green River Road. *GS/LPC/S.*

Ravenswood Manor (1913); Hart Place, also called Akin Park (1913); College Park and Lincolnshire (both 1923); Brookhaven (1928–32); and Arcadian Acres (1941)—private homes multiplied after World War II, with new suburban neighborhoods appearing in several parts of the city. Local builders Guthrie May and Gale Bradford were two of those who led the way; May built the first two prefabricated homes erected in Evansville on Bellemeade Avenue in 1946. Over the course of the next thirty years, his company constructed thousands of homes in Evansville, including the $1 million 100-home Lorraine Park (1948); Maplewood, advertised as "Evansville's newest restricted sub-division"[207] (1949); Washington Square (1950); Country Club Manor (1952); and Country Club Meadows (1956).[208] In his obituary in 1984, the buyer of a Guthrie May home in 1961 was quoted as saying, "Guthrie May made it possible for people like me to fulfill the American dream of home ownership."[209] Another local builder who shaped the postwar landscape was Gale Bradford, who was said to have built 3,000 homes in Evansville between 1937 and 1946. He built homes all across the East Side, including the 360-unit Columbia Apartments in 1946. In 1946–47, his company erected Iroquois Gardens between Lincoln

Iroquois Gardens under construction, 1947, looking west. Center left is Lincoln Avenue, center right is the State Hospital. *GS/LPC/S.*

Avenue and Division Street, the biggest subdivision in the city at that time and dubbed by his daughter-in-law "the Levittown of Evansville."[210] In the words of journalist Andrea Brown forty years later, "The 261-home Iroquois Gardens exemplified the then-phenomenon of tract subdivisions—tidy rows of Monopoly-type houses of simple geometrical design."[211]

Much of the early development was on the East Side, and by 1948, millions of dollars' worth of homes for over nine thousand people had been built there, turning an industrial section of the city into suburbia.[212] Subsequent development also included the North Side—Guthrie May's Country Club Manor, for example, with 563 lots by 1954, was by then nearly twice as large as any other subdivision in the city.[213] Development continued throughout the 1960s and 1970s, with important roles played by developers such as Wilfred C. "Bud" Bussing, who contributed to the birth of at least twelve subdivisions, including Fielding Court (1963), Evergreen Acres (1965) and Melody Hills (1965).[214] The expansion had spread east to the neighboring city of Newburgh, and by 1970, subdivisions were "springing up on all sides of Newburgh" as part of what one writer called a "residential boom in what is fast becoming Evansville's bedroom."[215]

Bottom left in this 1977 photo is Gale Bradford's Iroquois Gardens; center is Green River Road; top left is open space later occupied by the Eastland Mall. *EVPL.*

The housing revolution that saw thousands of people in Evansville buy their own homes and move to the suburbs was itself a reflection of what was happening all over the country. Americans moved to the suburbs in their millions in a social phenomenon that was shaped by a combination of intense demand for homes in a country of housing scarcity and an almost unlimited supply of money from federal assistance.[216] The latter point is worth emphasizing, as the expansion of the suburbs is sometimes characterized purely in terms of capitalist success or a builder's generous spirit—Guthrie May, for example, was said to have "began building north to make homes affordable for people who wanted to live there."[217] But none of it would have happened without two key components of the Roosevelt New Deal—the Home Owners' Loan Corporation (HOLC) of 1933 and the Federal Housing Administration (FHA) of 1934—that made mortgages much more secure and available and incentivized builders, buyers and lenders to play their parts in the process. Thirty-year mortgages became typical, and these mortgages, now guaranteed by the federal government, were more appealing since mortgage interest became tax-deductible.[218] This was then strengthened further after the war with the GI Bill of 1944 and the Veterans Administration (VA) that it set up.[219] In 1950, 1.7 million single-

Public housing in John F. Kennedy Towers. *EVPL.*

family homes were started—and the building never really stopped over the next two decades, conducted at a staggering pace.[220]

It was not just private housing that benefited from federal policy; public housing too was greatly encouraged and subsidized by the American Housing Act of 1949, which declared that every American deserved a "decent home and a suitable living environment" and whose Title III "committed the federal government to building 810,000 new public housing units."[221] It provided funds for the construction of public housing and was therefore strongly opposed by those who feared the competition it would provide; advertisements mass produced and circulated by the National Association of Home Builders and the U.S. Savings and Loan League appeared in both of Evansville's local papers in April 1952.[222] Their words were even parroted at a public debate at Evansville College in 1949, when realtor Harry Fitzgerald declared, "We think it's socialistic, we think it's political, we think it's expensive. And once you get it started, where are you going to stop?"[223] Undaunted by such opposition, the Evansville Housing Authority (EHA), which had been established by Mayor William Dress during the war, applied for and received hundreds of thousands of dollars from the Public Housing Administration and built hundreds of units of public housing, ranging from single-family homes to at least four high-rise blocks.[224] In 1953, 172 housing units at the Sweetser Homes were completed, to be followed by Erie Homes with 108 units in 1955 and Fulton Square with 120 in 1957. The 192 federally owned units at Lincoln Gardens came under the EHA in 1955. There were also 100 units in Kennedy Towers (1965) and 109 at Buckner Towers, dedicated in 1969.[225] In an interesting connection to the recent past, the Fulton Square development was on the site of a World War II federal housing project that had been totally demolished, with the exception of one office building, in 1952.[226] In 1972–73, the city added over 200 more units in two more high rises for the elderly: White Oak Manor and the William G. Schnute Towers. The impact was transformational—"I love it already… [but] I hope I live long enough to enjoy it," quipped the first resident of Schnute Towers in September 1972, while the first tenant at White Oak Manor declared in February 1973, "This is extraordinary grand, I'd run and jump if I could."[227]

While all of this housing expansion was a boon for those seeking accommodation, it needs to be emphasized that it was very much a racially segregated process across the country.[228] The suburbs, by and large, were to be for white people, as Black citizens, in the view of two recent writers, "found themselves systematically excluded from suburban residential locations by individual and institutional discrimination in the real estate and banking industries and by racially biased federal policies."[229] None of this was accidental, as the whole system was racist from top to bottom and was indeed designed to be so. According to the historian James A. Jacobs, "FHA policy itself was purposefully written in a way to exclude nonwhite Americans, using the abstract notion of 'market demands' as blanket justification for discrimination in sales. A prejudiced appraisal system for mortgages…further reduced access to the financial windfall that became available to white veterans and their families."[230] Furthermore, one of the most far-reaching actions of the HOLC in the 1930s was to conduct an "ambitious and secretive" initiative, the City Survey Program, to produce maps of 239 American cities with which they could assess the risk of issuing mortgages in particular places.[231] In his brilliant recent book, historian Richard Rothstein explained how the process worked: "The HOLC created color-coded maps of every metropolitan area in the nation, with the safest neighborhoods colored green and the riskiest colored red. A neighborhood earned a red color if African Americans lived in it, even if it was a solid middle class neighborhood of single family homes." [232] What this operation—now called redlining—did was send the message that Black people were too much of a risk to be given mortgages, and the areas so designated have in some cases suffered for almost nine decades.[233] The FHA followed this up by issuing their *Underwriting Manual* in 1936, which explicitly stated that a neighborhood could only maintain home values by retaining its social and racial makeup: "The infiltration of inharmonious racial groups...tend to lower the levels of land values and to lessen the desirability of residential areas."[234] Furthermore, the 1944 GI Bill was itself deeply flawed in terms of race and the VA benefits it delivered unequally distributed.[235] By these means—and all the ramifications that they bred—Black people were cut out from the single biggest social transformation of the twentieth century.[236]

It is important to note that all these things applied in Evansville too. In 1937, the HOLC mapped Evansville, along with several other significantly sized Indiana cities.[237] The resulting map designated seven areas of the city, 32 percent, as "Hazardous," including Baptistown. The "clarifying remarks" that went with the map described "two and three room shacks...all obsolete and lacking facilities. White labor mixed with probably 70 percent negro population." It also went on to mention "a Negro Low-Cost Housing Project...under construction."[238] This was to become Lincoln Gardens, a Black-only federal housing project that was constructed under the auspices of the PWA's Housing Division in 1936–38. What is striking about that project was that it was unlike what was done in cities like Atlanta and Miami, where Black families were displaced in the 1930s either to provide housing for white families or to expand the commercial area. As historian Robert G. Barrows observed, "In Evansville...community leaders sought to replace blighted housing in the midst of an African American district with vastly improved yet affordable housing in the same location.[239] Lincoln Gardens' first residents moved in in 1937, and the project was formally opened in the summer of 1938. It remained a significant part of the Black community for six decades until its demolition in 1997.[240]

It also remained a significant part of the segregation of Evansville, something that did not change after World War II. The postwar housing boom, both public and private, was racially segregated, and this segregation was sustained by Evansville realtors—as Black activist John M. Caldwell recalled in a 1973 interview, "The realtors had a gentleman's agreement that they wouldn't sell to Negroes in certain sections."[241] Realtors were a central part of this racist story nationwide, and indeed in the 1920s, the National Association of Real Estate Boards banned members from introducing "members of any race or nationality" whose "presence will clearly be detrimental to property values" in a particular neighborhood.[242] Segregation

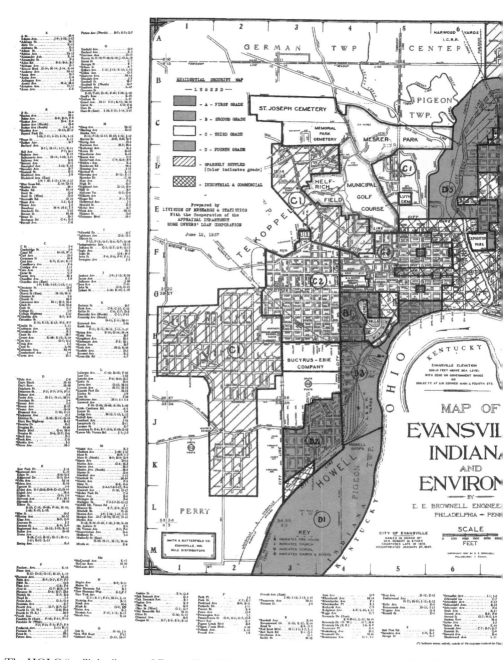

The HOLC "redlining" map of Evansville, 1937; red areas are marked with the letter D. *MI.*

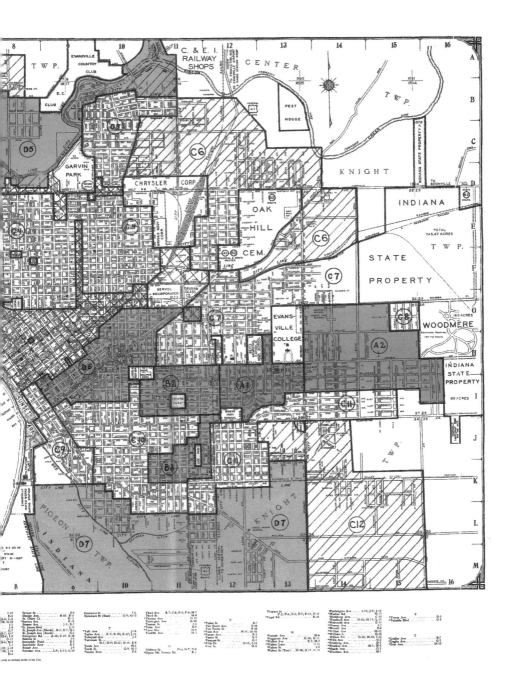

Lincoln Gardens federal housing project under construction, 1938. *USI.*

was often further sustained and enforced by restrictive covenants with language like this one recorded in Evansville in 1947:

> *The ownership and occupancy of lots and residents in this subdivision are forever restricted to those persons of the white Caucasian race, except that a white tenant or owner of any lot may permit his domestic servant or servants, not of the white Caucasian race, to occupy a room or rooms in his said residence building or a garage apartment during the time of such domestic service.*[243]

Eight years later, the *Evansville Press* ran an advertisement for the Vallamar Subdivision, a sixteen-home development on the city's southeast side, with the tagline "Evansville's FIRST Exclusive Subdivision for Colored." Iroquois Gardens had a stipulation, lasting until 1971, that none of it "shall be rented, leased, contracted to or conveyed to any other than those of Caucasian race."[244] None of this was new; Lincolnshire's 1923 covenant had similar racist language, as did a College Park Association covenant from

LINCOLNSHIRE, an Addition to the city of Evansville, Vanderburgh county, Indiana, as laid out by the proprietors thereof on lots one (1), eight (8) and the north half of lot number nine (9) in Shanklin's subdivision of the southwest quarter of section twenty-eight (28), township six (6) south, range ten (10) west, described and bounded as follows, to-wit: Commencing at the center of section twenty-eight (28), township six (6) south, range ten (10) west, which is the northeast corner of lot number one (1) in Shanklin's subdivision, extending thence south sixteen hundred and fifty (1650) feet, thence west 658.9 feet, thence north 1650 feet, thence east 653.7 feet to the place of beginning, names and width of streets, numbers and dimensions of lots, building lines and reservation for public utilities are shown on the plat attached. This plat is made subject to the following building and occupational restrictions:

1. All houses and outbuildings, including covered porches, shall be built within the building lines shown on this plat.

2. An easement for the use of all public utilities is reserved in the rear of lots as shown on this plat.

3. The building of residences only and proper outbuildings shall be permitted upon the lots in this plat.

4. No business structure of any kind may be erected nor shall any business, either mercantile or manufacturing, be carried on within the bounds of this plat.

5. All lots shall be kept clean.

6. No lot or improvement in this addition shall ever be sold, leased or rented to or contracted for in any way to a negro or negroes, nor shall ever be occupied by them, except those being domestic servants employed thereon or therein.

7. The foregoing limitations and restrictions shall operate in favor of each and all persons who shall from time to time respectively be the owner or owners of any lot or parcel of land in LINCOLNSHIRE and may be enforced by one or more of such parties by injunction or other proceedings in the event of a violation or attempted violation of any one of such limitations and restrictions or any part thereof by any person.

Joan R. Anderson
Henry B. Veatch

STATE OF INDIANA COUNTY OF VANDERBURGH: SS:

The Lincolnshire neighborhood's covenant containing racist language in restriction 6. *Eric Renschler.*

around the same period. The latter was eventually amended, but not until 1995.[245] Public housing, too, was restricted; when the federal government erected housing projects for war factory employees and their families in the city during World War II, they were segregated—five of the projects were for white people, and one, Mill Terrace, was for "Negro in-migrant war workers."[246] The Sweetser Homes of 1953 were designated to be for white people only until, in what has been called a "landmark housing discrimination lawsuit,"[247] this was challenged in federal court by two Black Evansville women. Jessie Woodbridge and Molly Bowling sued the EHA for a restraining order to prevent them from discriminating against Black people. They were backed by the local, state and national National Association for the Advancement of Colored Peoples (NAACP), and on July 6, 1953, Judge William E. Steckler ruled in their favor, saying, "It is unlawful for the Evansville Housing Authority to deny occupancy to eligible occupants where vacancies exist solely on the grounds of race or color."[248] The Evansville Human Relations Commission were active in the case too, as was John M. Caldwell, branch president of the Evansville NAACP. In a positive sign of the preservation and celebration of local history that could easily have been lost, the Sweetser Homes were renamed in 1987 in honor of Caldwell.[249]

The second big infrastructure effort the city made was urban renewal—a deliberate effort to eradicate blight, demolishing vast tracts of substandard structures in several parts of town. Urban renewal, a national and indeed worldwide phenomenon, came to Evansville in waves. Nationwide, the process disproportionately affected poor people and minorities. The activist

The condemnation of Pigeon Creek shacks in 1957. *EVPL.*

James Baldwin memorably said in 1963, "Urban renewal…means Negro removal."[250] It was funded by billions of federal dollars, and according to historian Francesca Ammon, "Roughly 7.5 million dwelling units were demolished between 1950 and 1980.…These demolitions reached their zenith in the 1960's, when wrecking crews tore down one out of every seventeen dwelling units nationwide."[251] The negative effects of these processes are reflected in some of the metaphors used to describe them: "the rape of our neighborhoods," "the slaughter of cities," "urban renewal as ethnic cleansing," "the sacking of cities" and "ruthless destruction."[252] The process also had the effect of reminding affluent Americans that poverty really existed, something that it was often easy for them to ignore, as Michael Harrington had written so famously in 1962: "The other America, the America of poverty, is hidden today in a way that it never was before. Its millions are socially invisible to the rest of us." [253]

In Evansville too, the process typically affected the poorest and most "invisible" part of the population. The very first action in Evansville was taken in early 1957 when about fifty structures on Pigeon Creek—houseboats and shanties—were condemned.[254] There had been shanties and houseboats there since at least 1901, when the *Journal* reported, "There are a number of shanties built near the water on the waste ground above the bridge.… The occupants are fishermen by occupation and the huts they live in are

High Street Slum Clearance Project. *WL.*

the merest shells of boards thrown together in a careless manner."[255] As has been seen, it became a sizable phenomenon during the Great Depression, and the encampment persisted into the 1950s. In 1955, a West Side Nut Club project led to the destruction of a number of the "wood and tar paper shacks," and by 1957, the city had decided to remove the homes there completely.[256] At the state level, the legal basis for urban renewal was the Indiana Redevelopment of Cities and Towns Act of 1953, and at a local level it was the Evansville Redevelopment Commission, established by an ordinance of the city council on May 4, 1953. The commission had the right to define properties as being in "a blighted area…[that] constitutes a menace to the social and economic interests of the City of Evansville and its inhabitants," acquire the properties if necessary by eminent domain, evict the occupants and demolish the buildings.[257] Although it was the first city to establish a redevelopment commission in Indiana, the process was mired in litigation for years, and the actual demolition of permanent structures did not get going until 1958.[258]

This undertaking, the High Street Area Slum Clearance Project, covered twenty-six city blocks on over 750 acres and saw the removal of some of the city's most notorious addresses, including the legendary red light district known variously as "Gear Town," "the District" and "the Line."[259] The existence of prostitution in the High Street area was an surprisingly open secret and a significant—if lost—part of Evansville life over the course of decades. Prostitution was being prosecuted in Evansville as early as 1874, and in 1876 the *Courier* reported that "the night police force made a raid on several houses of prostitution last night, and succeeded in bagging some very large game."[260] In 1906, the *Journal* discussed "the 'red light' district" as "a certain section along High and Lower First street where the greater number of dives of prostitution are now running unhindered," and indeed at that time Mayor John W. Boehne planned the "establishment of an official Red Light District" there. People complained about the proposal, and as the *Journal* reported, "They say that their homes would be destroyed and the value of their property considerably reduced by the presence of the obnoxious Red Light in their midst.[261] Half a century later, the same area was seeing the same activity: a 1953 story in the *Press* described "several months when sidewalks in the district were seldom empty, even during the early morning."[262] The slum clearance project lasted over five years and removed a mix of blighted residential and commercial structures, putting a mix of industrial and commercial buildings in their place. It was a successful effort, and by 1963, according to one local writer, the "showcase of the whole program, of course, is the High Street area. Once the center of the local prostitution industry, with unpaved streets, no sidewalks, and lots of crime, today it boasts a new name, paved streets, sidewalks, curbs and gutters, and land that is either cleared or else the site of new commercial and industrial buildings."[263] Prostitution, naturally, did not disappear and simply moved over the next few decades to locations like Fares Avenue and Haynie's Corner.[264]

This first urban renewal project also saw the multimillion-dollar expansion of Welborn Hospital and Welborn clinic, although there were also lots that were left empty, and some remain so over sixty years

The old downtown area before urban renewal in this 1937 photo; Old Courthouse is in the center. *USI.*

later. Officially, these first redevelopment efforts were termed Midtown Industrial Park, Riverside Project and Welborn Medical Center. The next initiative was the first project that saw residences demolished and replaced with new ones; this was in the Villa Sites area on the southeast side where some sixty-seven acres of substandard housing were removed and the new homes of Parkside Terrace took their place.[265] As late as 1955, Villa Sites was a neighborhood where there were people who lived in shacks with wooden floors, had no running water or inside plumbing and where an open sewer ran just feet from homes. There were rats, claimed Sam Elder, director of the Evansville sanitation department, which "went with dirt floors, no central heating, unsanitary water supplies and sewage deposited on the ground or in pit-type privies."[266] The Villa Sites project was a painfully elongated process; it started in the mid-fifties, but not a single family moved into replacement housing at Parkside until June 1972, by which time a paltry eleven homes had been built.[267] By April 1974, Parkside was finally virtually finished, complete with a park, tennis courts and a swimming pool, and with residents who were "pleased, almost blissful about their new homes and their new neighborhood."[268]

The old downtown area after urban renewal, 1970; Old Courthouse is top left. *USI*.

Other projects targeted a carefully selected group of rundown areas, and by the late 1970s, no fewer than twenty-seven separate redevelopment schemes had been carried out inside the city limits.[269] It can certainly be argued that while much of old Evansville was lost during this period, it needed to be done and the loss was unlamented. The demise of Villa Sites, for example, was marked with a mock funeral organized by the Redevelopment Commission and a condescending obituary on the front page of the *Courier*.[270] The loss of hundreds of acres of unsanitary slums and unsightly warehouses that would not have been out of place in Charles Dickens's London was in many ways a positive development for Evansville. And yet, it is naïve and patronizing to assume that the destruction of poor people's homes was without personal cost. A 1955 report in the *Courier* that highlighted the poor conditions in Villa Sites, for example, provoked a fascinating letter in response from one resident named Delores Daugherty. She pointed out that there were "very modern homes" there that did have inside plumbing, and she said,

> *We have moderate means but our home is ours. I pump water by hand, but*
> *if the city would bring water down Andover* [Avenue] *I'd be the first to*

Sunday Courier and Press

JUNE 2, 1968   EVANSVILLE, INDIANA   PAGE TWENTY-SEVEN—A

13 Buildings Down, 73 To Go

By HOMER ALLEY
Sunday Staff Writer

Dust — blinding, biting dust, removal a nearly a century old —is settling on a large part of downtown Evansville.

It is the dint of change.

For it spews from the wreckage of downtown buildings.

There's been a lot of dust and there will be a lot more. So far, the King Wrecking Co. has leveled 13 buildings and has 73 to go in the most ambitious urban renewal project undertaken by the city.

The project includes an eight and one-half block area bounded by Locust, Second and Ingle Streets and Riverside Drive.

The King Company has a $280,560 contract for clearing all buildings in the 26-acre Riverside Urban Renewal project.

Wrecking began on May 8. The resultant dust distances long litigation and endless paperwork dating from 1962.

Though the project was started on paper six years ago, the first actual purchase in the Riverside Renewal area was on May 3, 1967. Not until a year later were the first buildings going down.

Raymond A. Anderson, executive secretary of the Evansville Redevelopment Commission, says he anticipates "completion of acquisition of all property, including those parcels in condemnation proceedings, by Sept. 1, and completion of demolition by Dec. 11."

For some of the buildings, the wreckers does not come too soon.

Sometime during the first weekend after the wrecking started, one of the buildings on First Street, between Sycamore and Main, had failed structurally and one corner settled so violently the glass shattered in the front windows. Measurements showed the building had moved away from an adjacent building by one and one-half inches on the first floor and six inches on the third floor.

During condemnation proceedings an architect had testified that this building and adjacent buildings were weak and hazardous. He was right.

The cost of the land and buildings in the mammoth project is currently estimated at $4,161,300.

Anderson estimates that when the project is complete, the value of land in the area will be turn $1.8 million.

There is a difference of $-261,000.

"We are buying land and buildings and selling vacant land," Anderson explains.

The Federal Government is to pay three-quarters of the net cost and the local government is to pay one-quarter.

In addition to the cost of the land there is still to be add the cost of demolition and new curbs, gutters and sidewalks and mains street resurfacing.

Ultimately, Anderson expects the project to cost the Federal Government $3 million and the local government $1 million.

Redevelopment Commission plans call for use of the cleared land for "downtown retailing, including a department store, motor hotel, office buildings, high rise apartments and related commercial development," Anderson said.

A MAMMOTH HAND might have scooped away a half block area on Riverside Drive between Main and Locust Streets, but it was mere men with their machines.

A GIANT CLAMSHELL takes a neat with a mouth full of half-chewed beams, bricks and timbers while wrecking crews busy themselves with an electric line.

SIDEWALK CLOSED

NO EXAGGERATION is the sign warning of the obvious. When the wreckers working in the Riverside Redevelopment Project say the sidewalk is closed, they mean it.

THINGS MAY BE BAD, but never so bad that the Evansville Chamber of Commerce can't extend a cheerful welcome to visitors.

Welcome VISITORS

MAIN ST   SE 1 ST ST

What Will Rise Out of the Rubble?

What will rise from the rubble of the Riverside Renewal project?

At present, all indicators point toward a new plan for development from Victor Gruen Associates in the immediate future.

A conflict between the firm hired to come up with a master plan for revitalizing downtown Evansville and the Redevelopment Commission apparently has been settled.

Raymond A. Anderson, executive secretary of the Redevelopment Commission, said, "We have had a working meeting and substantial differences of opinion have been resolved."

He added that the original plans for the land still hold. He declined further comment on the June meeting.

The original plans call for the use of the cleared land for "downtown retailing, including a department store, motor hotel, office buildings, high rise apartments and related commercial development," according to Anderson.

Three tentative concepts for revitalizing the downtown area were presented in early March by the Gruen firm. None specified a use for the Riverside renewal land, nor did any provide for a department store in that area.

Shortly after Gruen's presentation, Redevelopment Commission officials charged that Frank McDonald and later Gruen Associates, at that time, said Gruen did not discuss plans with renewal personnel, or with the Plan Commission or with traffic engineering personnel in the city. He said he had taken reservations about Gruen's proposals.

Mayor McDonald said it said be ridiculous not to have the Gruen plan and redevelopment plans coordinated thoroughly.

Each must complement each other the mayor said. Each, he said, "will have to give a little and take a little, and we can come up with a highly successful redevelopment plan."

Mayor McDonald apparently has had his say.

If he has, we can expect a plan which relates the Riverside project to the revitalization of the downtown business district and a plan which coincides with the ones for the Riverside land as set forth by the Redevelopment Commission.

Urban renewal progress is monitored, June 1968. *EVPL.*

have it in my home. If the sewer came this way, I'm sure over 50% would make use of it....if Villa Sites property is a neglected area, who does the neglecting? Believe me, most of the children are not neglected and are just as fine as anyone else in Evansville.[271]

The letter reflects not just community identity and pride but also real anger directed toward those who did the neglecting and the landlords who owned the homes. "The run-down homes," wrote Daugherty, "are mostly owned by well-to-do men from downtown who don't care about this area and refuse to fix the homes up." She concluded,

Your article would do nothing but mislead a lot of people. There is a lot of ill feeling toward decent residents as it is and our children...[bear] the brunt of it, especially in high school. You parents teach your school children that children from Villa Sites are scum and therefore the children are slighted, etc. Is that fair? Don't you think it would have been much fairer to us if you had pictured both sides of Villa Sites?[272]

Over fifty years later, Muriel Essary recalled the neighborhood this way: "Everybody loved it. They were safe. The doors were never locked." Another former resident, Debbie Minor, said that Villa Sites was a place where people treated their neighbors like family: "The community always looked out for kids to make sure they had experiences they probably wouldn't have gotten otherwise."[273] More than just buildings were lost when the slums were cleared.

The third area of physical development to be considered in this chapter is roadbuilding, a process by which the city was eventually transformed, not just physically but arguably culturally, economically and psychologically too. These road projects reflect three hugely significant interconnected developments in American history that happened after World War II. The rise to dominance of the automobile, stimulated by the creation and expansion of the Interstate Highway system, led directly and inexorably to the relative decline of river transportation and the decline of the railroad. These changes had particular resonance for a city like Evansville, whose whole raison d'être for much of its history had been based on its relationship to the Ohio River. All this was to change after 1956, when the Interstate Highway system's construction accelerated greatly, with 90 percent of its funding coming from the federal government. While Evansville was not, strictly speaking, on an interstate in this period, nor were the roads built through it "freeways" in a technical sense, the roadbuilding that went on in

Columbia-Delaware Overpass opening ceremonies, March 1956. *EVPL.*

and around it can only be understood in that context. There was even talk in 1960 of Highway 41 being "brought into the federal Interstate system" although that never materialized, and I-64 did ultimately run just north of the city, but it was not until 2014 that a true interstate—I-69—eventually ran through the city.[274]

Surveys and planning began as early as 1950 for a new east–west expressway across Evansville, something that State Highway Commissioner A.J. Wedeking said would be "the most important highway development for Evansville since the Evansville-Henderson bridge was constructed [in 1932]."[275] The push to get this gained momentum in 1951 when the chamber of commerce set up a West Side Expressway Committee, representing many different interested groups. Wedeking said that "in no other city where the state highway department has contemplated major improvements have we received such whole-hearted cooperation as in Evansville." The development of the expressway was coordinated with the planning of a new Wabash River bridge west of Mount Vernon, and a route was selected in February 1952.[276] The first part of the "superhighway" opened in the summer of 1956, as did the $7 million bridge, and it was giddily predicted that the combination of the new bridge and the new expressway would lead to 80,000 industrial jobs in Evansville by 1970.[277] A further important step in tying together the East and West Sides of Evansville happened at the same time. In a complex and contentious process that started in 1953, a bridge was constructed over Pigeon Creek linking Delaware and Columbia Streets—the overpass was opened with great fanfare in March 1956 with a ceremony that featured dignitaries, West Side Nut Club members, the Mater Dei High School Band, a Marine Corps color guard and "half a dozen West Side dogs...[that] scampered through the crowd."[278] By 1963–64, discussions were in progress regarding the continuation of the expressway all the way east to Green River Road, with nine different routes considered.[279] In March 1965, the controversial decision was made, and the expressway was routed along the southern part of Division Street, keeping that street only as a service road. It was expected to have a profound impact on over 50 businesses in that area,[280] but moving forward was extremely complicated due to the need to remove trains and then railway lines from Division Street. The process was painfully slow and by 1969 had only progressed as far as the preliminary engineering stage. It dragged on throughout the 1970s, and what eventually became known as the Russell G. Lloyd Expressway was not finally completed until 1988. It had been a three-decade odyssey, during which the state acquired 492 property parcels and "paid for the relocation of 245 businesses, 357 residences, 34 signs, seven non-profit organizations and one farm....Acquisition cost totaled $35.7 million and relocations cost $4.2 million." The total cost of the Expressway was over $160 million.[281]

There were also numerous other roadbuilding projects that took place during this period, and at times many were happening simultaneously. The

Construction of the West Side Expressway bridge over Pigeon Creek, February 1956. Houseboats and shacks visible on the northeast side of the bridge. *EVPL.*

main north–south route through the city, Highway 41, was widened and in places rerouted in an enormous logistic undertaking that had its roots in the early 1950s and continued all the way through the mid-70s.[282] A combined riverfront boulevard and levee was constructed to ease traffic flow and simultaneously protect the city from the river in 1964, and a second major bridge across the river was added in 1965 beside the existing one at Henderson.[283] Diamond Avenue, another important east–west route across the city, was transformed—more or less—into an expressway in a multifaceted twenty-year project.[284] And the interstate system did come fairly close to Evansville when the east–west I-64 was built between 1962 and 1976. The location of the highway was bitterly contested, as its original 1947 route would have taken it through Vincennes, fifty miles north of Evansville.[285] After protests and lobbying and a prolonged process that lasted from 1957 to 1960, the U.S. Bureau of Public Roads finally announced its decision in June 1960. The route was moved farther south to just fifteen miles north of Evansville, with the bureau saying simply that this route would "best serve the purpose of the designated interstate."[286] The rerouting took a tremendous amount of effort from many different members of the Evansville community and was another example of Benjamin Bosse's "when everybody boosts, everybody wins" spirit.

Around the country and around the world, thousands of people rebelled and fought back against the impact that roadbuilding was having on their lives in a series of actions collectively known as highway revolts.[287] Of their many spokespersons, one of the most articulate was the influential urban critic Lewis Mumford, who said in 1958,

> *Perhaps our age will be known to the future historian as the age of the bulldozer and the exterminator; and in many parts of the country the building of a highway has about the same result upon vegetation and human structures as the passage of a tornado or the blast of an atom bomb. Nowhere is this bulldozing habit of mind so disastrous as in the approach to the city....As a consequence the "cloverleaf" has become our national flower and "wall-to-wall" concrete the ridiculous symbol of national affluence and technological status.*[288]

While Mumford's words certainly have relevance when looking at Evansville, the city did not experience a large-scale "revolt" against roadbuilding. The experiences of several Evansville groups, however, are a reminder of the struggles that surrounded large-scale urban roadbuilding projects in this period.

In a situation that dragged on from 1954 to 1956, residents of the 1900 block of Delaware Street fought the city for compensation after a massive concrete wall ended up in front of their properties as a result of the Columbia-Delaware Overpass. Ten households ended up receiving $17,900 each from the city in damages.[289] In 1955, a number of residents complained about the nature of the intersection of Third Avenue and the Expressway; 449 signed a petition to the Mayor's Traffic Commission asking that Third Avenue remain as an uninterrupted north–south route.[290] The State Highway Commission, however, refused to make any changes to the plans, and Third Avenue lost its status as a north–south arterial route. And then in 1957 the homeowners on the 3400 block of Corbierre Avenue started a protest over diminished property values after an expressway overpass was built in front of their homes. In a letter to the Indiana Highway Commission, they claimed that they "face a wall of dirt up to 20 feet high which shuts out view, air,

Opening ceremony for the West Side Expressway, June 1956. *EVPL.*

drainage and interferes with TV reception." It was a similar situation to the one that had come up in 1954, and homeowners indeed cited the example of the Delaware Street property owners as being "similarly damaged."[291] Initially rejected, they appealed to the attorney general, who examined their case but rejected it on the grounds that "under present decisions of the courts an abutting owner is not entitled to compensation for any alleged damage."[292] While it is important to note that none of these protests were against roadbuilding per se and none of them succeeded in stopping the roads themselves, they remind us that for many people in this period—in Evansville and countless other places—road construction projects represented loss rather than benefit.

The fourth and final aspect of infrastructure development in this period was the construction of key public buildings of many different kinds, a process that shaped Evansville as much as anything else discussed in this book. Two of these buildings were iconic structures that were to play a substantial part in Evansville's cultural life for the next fifty years: Roberts Municipal Stadium in 1956 and a new Evansville Museum in 1959.[293] The push for a stadium began in earnest in the early 1950s, with various scenarios considered. By 1953, the site had been selected and the city council approved a $1 million bond issue to finance the project. On March 18, 1955, Mayor Hank Roberts posed for photographs at the official groundbreaking, and by October 1956 the stadium was finished.[294] On October 28, the first event was staged, when around 9,000 watched the Harlem Globetrotters, "the fabled Negro team" in the words of the *Press*, and a vaudeville show at the stadium. A few weeks later, 10,500 fans packed the building on dedication night to watch the Evansville College men's basketball team lose in the final seconds to Purdue, and a tempestuous five-decade love affair between the building and the city had begun.[295] The stadium was demolished in 2013, and while a large grassy space is all that remains at the site, some memories of Roberts Stadium are preserved in a "Corridor of Champions" at the downtown stadium that replaced it.

The Evansville Museum began its modern life in the old YMCA building on Second Street, but as early as 1937 there was a campaign to move to a new building with an auditorium and a theater, to "build for the city a fitting edifice in which to house the rapidly-expanding museum of Arts, Sciences, and history."[296] Given the timing, nothing was to happen for more than a decade, but by the early 1950s the possibilities began to stir anew. Given urgency by the unsuitability of the existing museum, eyes began to settle on Sunset Park as a location—the site of the city's earliest attempt at running a museum—and the museum's energetic young director Siegfried Weng led the charge. On July 30, 1953, for the sum of $1 per year, the Park Board granted a fifty-year lease of much of Sunset Park as a site for the Museum.[297] After four years of discussions and delays, with slight modifications to both the submitted plans and the lease, the Park Board (now belonging to a different administration) finally approved the $600,000 project.[298] Ground was broken on a bitterly cold day in December 1957, and the museum opened to the public on October 18, 1959. The most popular attractions included an Alaskan brown bear, which still enthralls visitors, and the "mummified…remains of a Southwestern Indian maiden who died about 700 A.D."—which, in a sign of a more enlightened time, is no longer a feature of the museum.[299] Today the museum continues to thrive and helps ensure that Evansville's history is not lost; indeed, probably no institution in the city has done more to preserve Evansville's past.

The public library system expanded significantly with the dedication of several newly constructed branch libraries. The twelve-thousand-square-feet McCollough Library on Washington Avenue, named for Ethel F. McCollough, who was head librarian from 1912 to 1947, was built in

Construction of Roberts Municipal Stadium, 1956. *USI.*

The start of construction at the new Evansville Museum, 1958. *USI.*

The new North High School nears completion, 1956. *EVPL.*

1964–65 and opened in July 1965. Meadow Park was built, after a two-year struggle over funding, to provide services for the people who had moved into Guthrie May's north side developments. The eleven-thousand-square-foot building was opened in December 1968. After two years of extensive renovation, the Oaklyn branch library in the former Lynch Elementary School, built in 1930, opened for borrowers in January 1975.[300] Schools, too, saw new construction. In 1956, North High School was built, the "first new public secondary educational institution in the city since Lincoln, built in 1929,"[301] and this was followed in 1962 by a new East Side high school, William Henry Harrison, an example of "modern school planning, with a complex of buildings, open courts, and miles of glass walls." A new Central High School—ironically built north of North High School—opened in 1971. In addition, ten new elementary schools were constructed, and at least twenty had additions built, as well as several parochial schools.[302] It is noteworthy that here, as with so much else, Evansville is both a unique case study and an absorbing reflection of nationwide phenomena. It is not surprising to see so many public schools built in Evansville when this too was happening everywhere—in 1989, 61 percent of the public schools in the United States had been built in the 1950s and 1960s, and even seven years later, according to the U.S. Department of Education, that number had only fallen to 50 percent.[303] The postwar baby boom meant that a decade later all these children were entering the school system and there was a desperate shortage of space.

Colleges grew massively in the United States in this period too. While not a public institution, Evansville College saw enormous expansion after World War II as the GI Bill and other social changes brought students flocking. Buildings exploded over the campus throughout the next twenty years as the college enjoyed the greatest growth in its history. As well as an abundance of student housing and residence halls, the college built McCurdy Alumni Memorial Union (1951), Clifford Memorial Library (1957), Krannert Hall, Wheeler Concert Hall, Carson Center (all 1962), Harper Dining Center (1964), Neu Chapel (1966), Hyde Hall and Shanklin Theater (both 1967).[304] In February 1967, Evansville College became the University of Evansville, but by then the city had already welcomed a second university that would eventually become the University of Southern Indiana: Indiana State University–Evansville (ISUE) was established in the fall of 1965. Initially using the old Centennial School building, in 1966 the institution acquired a large tract of land on the far West Side and ground was broken for the brand-new campus in June 1968. The Administration-Science building (1969) was the first to be erected,

The first buildings begin to appear at the ISUE campus, 1972. *EVPL.*

The futuristic proposal for a "Civic Circle," 1963. *WL.*

followed by the Temporary Union Building (1970), the University Library (1971) and the University Center (1974). The Technology Center was opened in the fall of 1975.[305]

But by far the biggest building project undertaken in Evansville during this time was the construction of a massive new Civic Center complex downtown to house both county and city government as well as courts, a jail, police and sheriff's department headquarters, a federal building, the headquarters of the school corporation, a post office and a convention center–auditorium. Many alternative ideas came and went over the decades before the eventual plan was formed, one of which has captured the popular imagination ever since. This was the so-called Civic Circle, which was proposed and received with great enthusiasm in 1963; the architects' plan called for the buildings in the complex to form a spectacular and elegant circle, with traffic flowing around them. The expressway was planned to run alongside, and, if built, Evansville would have looked like something from the Futurama model at the 1939 New York World's Fair.[306] The dreams lasted only a few months, however, and by July a different architectural firm proposed a much more mundane campus-style layout, commenting dryly of the circle, "It would have certain drawbacks. It may be that another solution is better."[307] The Civic Circle was gone. Once "another solution" crystalized and the precise location was decided, the process to acquire the three key pieces of real estate was both complicated and fortuitous. But in the end, the C&EI Railroad sold its thirteen-acre rail yard, owner Tony Hulman sold the closed Cook Brewery and Bishop Henry Grimmelsman, on behalf of the Roman Catholic Church, sold Assumption Cathedral.[308] The Civic Center project could now proceed, and there was enormous excitement and optimism about what it meant—a *Courier* editorial termed it "the beginning of a more extensive project to revitalize the entire downtown area," and when ground was symbolically broken in June 1966 by Evansville mayor Frank McDonald, he claimed that the development would be "the beginning of a downtown revitalization without equal in American cities the size of Evansville." The Civic Center was completed in 1969 at the cost of $25 million and was formally dedicated in an elaborate ceremony spread over two days, attended by Indiana governor Edgar Whitcomb, U.S. senator Vice Hartke and countless other dignitaries. An open house for the general public, with tours, guides and a twenty-minute slide show running every half hour, was attended by thirty to thirty-five thousand people, at least one of whom got to sit in the mayoral chair and declare the place "Fantastic." One visitor said, "I feel differently about the cost, now that I've had the chance to

Looking up Main Street at the newly completed Civic Center complex. *EVPL.*

see it. I think it's all beautiful."[309] Looking beyond the physical, journalist Homer Alley declared that it "marked the completion of the most massive single forward motion in the history of Evansville."[310]

This whole project was rendered even more complex and significant by the planning, land purchases and "the largest demolition project in Evansville history" on an over forty-acre site that had had to precede it.[311] In 1966, the *Sunday Courier and Press* declared in a celebratory tone,

> *The clearing away of the old is about done and the flinging up of the new is the order of the day. There is more razing to be done, of course.… The Welborn Baptist Renewal Area is in the demolition stage now. And there's the Riverside Renewal area, still in litigation. A 9½-block area is to be cleared of all but a few structures, then sold to developers, meaning that rickety and eye-sore-like buildings are to be replaced by gleaming new edifices. Among them are expected to be high-rise apartments, commercial and office buildings, and motels or hotels, or both.*[312]

None of this considered the cost, and the loss, to Evansville of "the clearing away of the old." At least three iconic Evansville structures were demolished to make way for the beautiful brutalism of the Civic Center Complex, with a fourth following to provide parking spaces. Assumption Cathedral (1872) and the F.W. Cook Brewery (rebuilt 1891) were razed in 1965, and the old C&EI Railway Terminal, built in 1907 and used as the white USO club during World War II and as the city's community center thereafter, came down the following year.[313] The oldest high school in the city, Central (1868), saw its students relocated in 1971 and, after a failed effort to at least save its 1898 tower, was leveled in 1973.[314] In an eloquent elegy to the cathedral on the day of its final mass, James F. Ellis described the ring of its bell that morning as "a long mournful toll, more a death knell than a call to worship." Then he said,

> *The massive structure at 7th and Vine has withstood floods and fires and been intertwined with the history and growth of Evansville since its cornerstone was set in place July 7, 1872, but now progress, in its odd way, has demanded its destruction. Demolition will begin in February or March. But where the cathedral must die, a city will be reborn. The site will become a part of the proposed Civic Center complex and will provide land for the new federal court and office building.*[315]

The demolition of the Cook Brewery, 1964. *EVPL.*

In stark contrast to Ellis's sanguine and poetic reaction, parishioners were extremely unhappy at the toll that "progress" demanded. "So many people I've talked to feel it's such a crime…such a terrible crime to tear down such a beautiful church," said Anna Keller, while Clyde Vize, who had been a parishioner for almost sixty years, said, "It's just a dirty

Demolition of Assumption Cathedral, with the Central High School tower behind, 1965. *USI.*

shame that it has to be destroyed."[316] A third member of the Cathedral congregation, John Payne, could have been speaking for the whole city as it reflected on the creative destruction of the period when he observed, "Most of us feel it's a bitter pill to swallow and I think Evansville will eventually realize that it has lost an important facet of its culture with the passing of the Cathedral."[317]

What Ellis's remark—"where the cathedral must die, a city will be reborn"—perfectly reflects is the essential connection between demolition and construction. In this era, it seemed that one could only proceed in conjunction with the other. It was all quite simple: urban scholar Martin Anderson wrote in 1964 that the way urban renewal worked was to "change one kind of neighborhood into another kind by destroying the old buildings and replacing them with new ones."[318] Historian Francesca Ammon has said that the prevailing attitude was "creative destruction—to achieve progress we

Down comes the tower of Assumption Cathedral, 1965. *USI.*

needed to destroy that which came before to make way for this new building. Rather than looking to old built fabric as something that could be restored or improved, we're actually going to destroy it to make something anew." A 1965 photo essay in the *Sunday Courier and Press* was titled simply and starkly, "Construction and Destruction." At the Civic Center groundbreaking, one writer tied the two processes together elegantly: "A new era in the city's life began today as an old one crumbled away in the background....As a crowd of officials and community leaders looked on at the ground-breaking ceremony, a crane worked away in the background tearing down a building of another era."[319] As the architecture writer Jeff Byles has pointed out, when new buildings go up in an urban environment, they almost always require that the already existing buildings on the site be demolished.[320] This was inevitably true in Evansville also: the Cook Brewery was demolished to build the Civic Center complex, but in 1890 the *Journal* reported that Cook had bought some property at Seventh and Main and said, "It is understood that the present buildings will be removed after awhile when an elegant brewery building will take their place."[321] "What happened during 1969 was that a great number of old and generally useless buildings were erased from the landscape," observed a *Courier* reporter cheerfully. "Their replacement with new facilities will provide the look of the 70s."[322] In the view of the historian Gary Schwartz, "The federal urban renewal legislation of 1954 had rested on the basic premise that slums were in essence a problem of deteriorated buildings, rather than a problem of the low-income of those buildings' inhabitants. The solution, therefore, was to tear down these buildings and replace them with structures housing useful civil activities."[323] Evansville embraced this creative destruction, it seemed, with almost limitless zeal.

Creative destruction was symbolized above all else by the bulldozer. As Francesca Ammon argued, "In both its physical and cultural manifestations, the bulldozer dramatically transformed the postwar American landscape.... The bulldozer was the iconic instrument of and symbol behind this transformation."[324] In 1968, the Evansville redevelopment process was summarized by the phrase "the urban renewal bulldozer,"[325] and in 1975, when considering the "urban renewal issue," *Evansville Press* journalist Roberta Heiman could capture the whole issue with the simple rhetorical question, "Is bulldozer [the] only answer?"[326] When workers broke ground on the new Civic Center in June 1966, Mayor Frank McDonald was photographed wearing a hard hat while at the controls of a bulldozer. Even when the mayor was not available, somebody else would step in to be photographed on a symbolic bulldozer—when the next stage of the Villa Sites demolition began in Evansville in September 1968, the city council president came forward to "mount a bulldozer, signaling the official beginning of the end for Villa Sites."[327] Additionally, in Evansville bulldozers were close to the community's heart, as International Harvester and Bucyrus-Erie were both big players in the bulldozer game and big names in local industry.[328] For others in

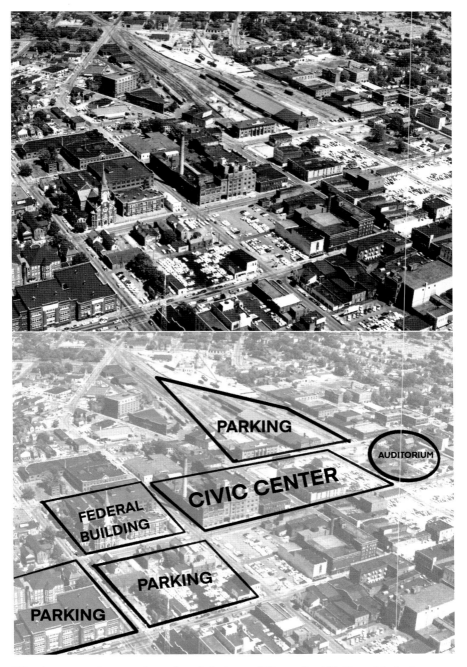

The almost complete transformation of the heart of Evansville. *WL/James MacLeod.*

Downtown, circa 1973. The Auditorium, Civic Center and Federal Building are all complete, and whole blocks by the river have been cleared. Middle right is Central High School, awaiting demolition. *USI.*

Evansville, however, the bulldozer and the changes that it symbolized were a source of fear. Journalist Roberta Heiman met with the Black residents of the run-down Oakdale neighborhood in 1971, and said, "They fear the threat of an urban renewal bulldozer coming in and destroying their homes, their community, everything they value."[329]

Therefore, as Evansville faced the second half of the 1970s, there was much to look forward to, much to celebrate and much that had been lost. Some were happy; some were not. Journalist Homer Alley called the dedication of the Civic Center "a dramatic conclusion [to] a...dream for a revitalized Evansville. The $27 million project is the keystone of the new Evansville."[330] Another writer, David M. Berry, looked back on the McDonald mayoral regime and declared that "McDonald has been able to accomplish what many other mayors only dream about."[331] While some saw it all as the stuff of dreams, others, like architectural critic William Morgan, were far from impressed:

Except for a pedestrian shopping mall…and a few mostly prewar tall buildings, the center of down-town Evansville looks like it has been bombed. One is afraid to ask what used to be on all these open spaces and parking lots. It is almost as if the town fathers have eradicated the city's history in a frenzied effort to provide parking in order to compete with suburban shopping malls.[332]

These two divergent views serve as an appropriate conclusion to a discussion of Evansville's infrastructure changes during this period. They also serve as a reminder of how divided perspectives were during one of the most turbulent and divisive periods in American history. It is to a study of the cultural divides in Evansville, especially those around race, that we now finally turn.

4

While 1945–75 was a period that shaped today's United States in numerous ways, it was one that straddled two very different realities—the immediate post–World War II era of American confidence and optimism, and the post-Watergate era of doubt and disillusionment. It was a period of bewildering and momentous change and challenge, as the country witnessed the Korean War, the Red Scare, the Kennedy Camelot, the Cuban Missile Crisis, the Watergate scandals, the civil rights movement, the Vietnam War and the antiwar movement, the youth movement, hippies and yippies, the birth of environmentalism, the women's movement, the space race that put U.S. astronauts on the moon, the *Roe v. Wade* decision and the assassinations of John F. Kennedy, Malcolm X, Dr. Martin Luther King and Senator Robert Kennedy. All of this, and much more besides, had to be absorbed and interpreted by the people of Evansville. Some of the most challenging aspects of this period for the city came from the so-called counterculture, and despite the city's sometimes sleepy image, the fact that the counterculture existed and at times thrived in a heartland city like Evansville should not be surprising. What the historian Beth Bailey wrote about the sexual revolution could be applied to the whole countercultural movement: "Despite the way it is often portrayed in contemporary diatribes and debates, the sexual revolution was not created by a set of radicals on the fringe of American society and then imposed on the rest of the nation. It was forged in America's heartland as well."[333]

A time of challenge. A young man with an upside-down flag at the Bull Island music festival, 1972. *USI.*

Evansville people, for example, took illicit drugs. Local media reports on this ranged from a breathless front-page story in 1956 revealing that a local juvenile delinquent could get "marijuana cigarettes any time he wants them from a West Side gang" to a 1973 story in which a local drug dealer estimated that there were "easily 10,000 regular users of marijuana in Evansville." Shockingly, he also added that "there are even a few cops who smoke grass."[334] Jimi Hendrix played Roberts Stadium in June 1970, finishing his set with "The Star-Spangled Banner" and "Purple Haze," and Alice Cooper played there to over 11,000 in March 1975.[335] An estimated crowd of 100,000 to 300,000 people from all over the country attended the chaotic Bull Island music festival on Labor Day weekend in 1972. Journalist Rich Davis said of the event, about twenty-five miles from Evansville, "The counterculture was staging three days of music, love and peace in a lawless setting."[336] Students on the Evansville College campus publicly debated obscenity laws and abortion in January 1972, while the following week's topic was "Jesus—The Great Psychic."[337] In 1972, two people were charged with

109

The counterculture comes to town: the Bull Island music festival, September 1972. *USI.*

obscenity for running an adult bookstore on Main Street, leading to the store being closed down.[338] There was even a local commune called Padanaram founded in 1966 in rural Martin County, about one hundred miles from Evansville, where scores of people lived in what their leader Daniel Wright called "a nation within a nation."[339]

Central to much of the social and cultural divide in America was the Vietnam War, which the historian David Steigerwald called "the defining event of the sixties, for it reflected and pronounced the wider social currents in all their ambiguity."[340] By the war's end, around 58,000 Americans had been killed and over 150,000 wounded; at least 1 million Vietnamese were killed.[341] The war affected Evansville from almost the very beginning of hostilities, with the first local casualty occurring on July 10, 1964. Leonard Lockard was a nineteen-year-old helicopter door gunner, killed when his aircraft was shot down less than two months into his tour of duty. His son was just six days old.[342] In the end, 67 Evansville men were killed, including graduates of all the local high schools: 11 from Bosse, 11 from North, 10 from Reitz, 7 from Central, 6 from Harrison, 5 from Rex Mundi and 1 each from Memorial and Mater Dei. The bodies of men from surrounding areas who were killed in Vietnam were flown into Evansville airport.[343] In addition to those killed, many other local men were wounded. Bill Collins, for example, was a navy medic who joined up shortly after graduating from North High School. In February 1969, he lost part of his shoulder and suffered multiple shrapnel wounds while treating an injured marine; he was subsequently burned, shot, stabbed and hit by a mortar explosion during the same incident. He said that he did not know how he survived, explaining, "I guess it just wasn't my time."[344] Another local man, Gary May, was a young marine and described the experience of being wounded in early 1968 in a memorable 2009 interview:

> It turned out one of the places that I chose to cross [the dike] was a spot that had been mined. I stepped on what was a pressure detonated mine… and it released, it triggered the explosion, and I was thrown up into the air. I don't know how far, but I have fairly vivid memories of some of the things that I saw at the time including, you know, this image of my left boot with my foot still in it taking off from my body at about a forty-five-degree angle from the explosion.…I wasn't fully aware of the extent of my injuries initially. When I started to get up, I lifted or pulled the trunk of my body forward to get up, and it was quickly apparent to me that I didn't have any counter balancing weight at the bottom, because my legs were gone.[345]

Evansville's memorial commemorating the city's Vietnam War dead. *James MacLeod.*

Both men survived but suffered much both physically and mentally as a consequence of their injuries. Gary May has been an indefatigable advocate for peace in the decades following his injury and has done much to ensure that the Vietnam War's terrible effects are not lost to history.

The war was one of the deepest social and cultural fault lines in the country, and Evansville did not escape this division. The city saw antiwar demonstrations, often led by students from both UoE and ISUE, such as the November 1969 Candlelight March downtown or the May 1970 Antiwar Ball on the UoE campus. In 1970, UoE students took part in a nationwide petition campaign that declared "We Won't go." Some young people made the decision to register as a conscientious objector (CO), difficult as that was; Rob Spear of Evansville recalled,

> *When I turned eighteen, I registered CO. I vividly remember sitting at our dining room table telling my father. It brings tears to my eyes thinking about it. I told him the war was wrong and I wasn't going. It was a really really hard conversation. I remember seeing my dad's face when I told him I wasn't going to Vietnam. He was crushed; he didn't want me to be in*

"harm's way" but he wanted me to support my country, like he did during Korea. I said that I'd do anything but I wasn't going to kill. At the end, I think he realized and respected my dedication to peace.[346]

University faculty also spoke out—"Violence begets violence," declared UoE History professor Thomas Fiddick at a 1970 peace rally where fellow professors Don Richardson, Wayne Perkins and Phillip Ott all spoke too.[347] Fiddick, indeed, wrote a letter to the editor of the *Press* as early as January 1965 condemning the war and calling for U.S. withdrawal, and he spoke out in a campus debate and on TV later that year.[348] At the height of the war, the presence of Reserve Officers' Training Corps (ROTC) became controversial on many college campuses, and in 1969 the countercultural weekly paper at UoE, *The Iconoclast*, urged "the faculty and administration to institute courses on waging peace with similar credit as found in ROTC courses, or else to remove college credit from ROTC courses."[349] In May 1970, at Ohio's Kent State University, the ROTC building was burned down and the National Guard was deployed on campus; on May 4, guardsmen shot live rounds into a crowd of student antiwar protesters. Four young people were killed in one of the most momentous of all the culture-clash incidents of the era. John Filo's stunning and Pulitzer Prize–winning photograph of a young woman kneeling over the body of one of the dead students was featured the next day on the front page of the *Courier*, while the *Press* used another of Filo's photos on its front page.[350] In the next few days, 175 local students demonstrated peacefully at the downtown federal building and police stood guard at the UoE ROTC building amid rumors of an arson attack. The building was indeed attacked, but with only stencils and paint—neat blue swastikas were painted on the ROTC signs. On May 8, students at a Kent State memorial rally on the UoE campus scuffled with another group of students over a flag flying at half-staff. Meanwhile passing motorists honked and yelled, "Get a haircut, you hippies!" at the students, and a letter to the editor in the next edition of the UoE newspaper condemned the protesters, declaring, "Go some place else. We don't want them."[351] At an earlier Evansville student-led protest march, in November 1969, one observer "expressed a desire 'to kill some of those protesters.'"[352]

These last three examples are an important reminder that a significant portion of Americans supported the Vietnam War or at least opposed the antiwar movements; they were members of Richard Nixon's so-called silent majority.[353] It is important therefore to emphasize that "culture" in this period is not limited to a study of the counterculture; on a 1973

John Filo's photograph on the front page, May 1970. *EVPL.*

Courier front page that carried an account of twenty arrests at a Roberts Stadium rock concert, the main story was about thirty-eight arrests at the Press Club's annual bierstube, an event that could hardly have been less countercultural.[354] Therefore, Evansville is an enlightening case study in that it showcases both the counterculture and the mainstream culture that was being rebelled against, a very important component of the culture not just of Evansville but of the United States as a whole.[355] The mainstream culture in the city included such things as high school and college athletics, especially football and basketball, the West Side Nut Club Fall Festival, theater, movies, the Evansville Philharmonic orchestra and the various activities and influences of first one and then two universities. Above all, perhaps, religion—specifically Christianity—retained a prominent place in Evansville social life. Through the 1940s and up until 1955, for example, the *Evansville Press* on Saturdays carried a listing of the topics of upcoming Sunday sermons. In January 1955, it listed ninety-two different Protestant congregations in fifteen categories, while twenty years later, the paper was still advertising Protestant services at eighty-five separate locations, divided into twenty-seven categories.[356] This does not even include others such as Roman Catholics, Jews and Muslims. In 1969, on the twenty-fifth anniversary of the Catholic Diocese of Evansville, it was estimated that there were 83,000 communicants in sixty-nine parishes and 130 priests. There were two Jewish congregations during this period: Washington Avenue Temple and Adath Israel. They thrived in the early years, but numbers were dwindling by the 1970s and the two merged in 1980. The Muslim community was small, with only an estimated 150 members as late as 1995.[357] Given all that, it is clear that there were two cultures that clashed in Evansville between 1960 and 1975, and while events in Evansville were not always quite as dramatic as they were in some other places, these movements and the debates they involved were very much part of life. At times, the divisions were stark.

Nothing, however, revealed the stark division in American society in the postwar period like race—"the longest and most painful drama this country has known," according to Barack Obama biographer David Remnick.[358] Race was certainly a long and painful drama in Evansville, and therefore the focus of the rest of the chapter is the complexities of racial division in the city, a topic that has been at times lost in the telling of the Evansville story. It was lost even though racism was often right there in front of people's eyes; it was certainly clear to see for John M. Caldwell, the first Black person elected to the city council, who said in 1973, "Evansville at heart is a racist town."[359] Often, however, it seemed that white people remained unable—or unwilling—to acknowledge it. In July 1964, a burning cross appeared on the lawn of the overwhelmingly Black Lincoln School. It is revealing that the *Evansville Press* immediately blamed "pranksters"— putting the words "Pranksters Blamed" *above* the headline and having as its lede, "A burning cross, believed to the work of pranksters, was found last night on the lawn of Lincoln School."[360] There was no discussion of underlying issues or analysis of root causes. This chapter, then, discusses four areas of race-related contention in Evansville during this period: acts of violence and disorder, the fight over school desegregation, the journey to integration of public facilities and the struggle for an open housing ordinance. Before all that, however, it is important to discuss some of the painful historical context that set the scene for the explosive race-related developments of the period from 1955 to 1975.

There were Black people in Evansville from almost the very beginning, some of whom were enslaved, and according to historians Tamara Hunt and Donovan Weight, "The 1850 census showed that there were 230 'free Colored' citizens—two percent of the population. This number grew rapidly,

The lynching of Bud Rowland and Jim Henderson in Rockport, Indiana, December 1900. Five white onlookers pose for the camera. *USI.*

in part because…one route for escaping slaves went through Evansville and ran along the Wabash and Erie Canal."[361] The city has celebrated its role in the Underground Railroad—Willard Carpenter, for example, is frequently and correctly lauded for his role in that system, and rumors persist about the role of an underground tunnel running from his house to the river.[362] But by many measures, Black residents in Evansville do worse than white residents even today, and the darker side of Evansville's past—the racism—has been largely and conveniently lost.

Two Black men were lynched in Evansville in 1865, and this incident remains the only example of race-based lynching in the city's history. It should be stated, however, that in 1903 a significant race riot was born out of an attempted lynching, and there were horrific lynchings in neighboring communities. Seven Black men—Jim Good, Jeff Hopkins, Ed Warner, William Chambers, Dan Harris Sr., Dan Harris Jr. and John Harris—were lynched in Mount Vernon in 1878 in the biggest mass lynching in Indiana history. December 1900 saw the lynchings of three Black men by white mobs in two nearby towns: Bud Rowland and Jim Henderson in Rockport and Joe Holly in Boonville. The 1865 Evansville lynching was in response to the alleged rape by two Black men of a white woman named Mrs. Dullinger. According to the first local newspaper account, "The whole neighborhood was quickly aroused and turned out in search of the fiends." Two Black men—one named Joe Goins and the other unnamed—were arrested and held in the city's jail. "This revolting outrage," concluded the article, "has created much feeling in the city, and the infamous and brutish wretches will no doubt receive, as they deserve, the severest punishment of the law."[363] The law, however, was not to be allowed to run its course, as the very next day the same paper reported,

> *The two negro brutes, who so fiendishly maltreated a white woman on Sunday, fearfully expiated their crime yesterday afternoon....They were soon dragged forth into the street, beaten down with clubs and shot. After they were dead they were taken up and hanged to a lamp post on the corner of the street, where they were* [still] *hanging at a late hour in the evening.*[364]

The dehumanization in the language—"fiends," "fiendishly," "brutish," "brutes"—is crystal clear and was typical of press accounts of lynchings in the United States. Black lynching victims, it was made clear, were nothing more than animals; indeed an account of the Evansville lynching on the front page of the *Chicago Tribune* literally called the victims "inhuman scoundrels."[365] One day later, acting mayor Samuel Orr issued a proclamation condemning the lynch mob and pointing out that one of the dead men, "it is believed, on the testimony of the outraged woman, was innocent of any connection to the crime."[366] The incident, part of a much more generalized pattern of anti-Black violence in Indiana and across mostly the American South,[367] was widely reported at the time, and its provenance was clear to the *Vincennes Sun*—which interpreted it as "a warning to [N-word]s in this part of the State [to] keep their place, and keep it well, or they will be exterminated."[368] The incident was acknowledged by one early historian, but subsequent general histories of Evansville have chosen to ignore the incident and it has not been discussed in local media for decades. It is, in many respects, lost history.

The city jail, scene of start of the Evansville Race Riot in 1903. *James MacLeod*.

The 1903 race riot is a better documented piece of Evansville's dark racial history, mentioned in most of the general histories and fairly frequently in local media. On July 4, a white policeman, Louis Massey, was shot and killed, and the Black man who killed him, Lee Brown, was locked up in the Evansville jail until being transferred to Vincennes for his own safety; chaos and disorder ensued. The *Journal-News* declared on the front page that the city was "in the Hands of a Desperate Mob. Race Feeling at High Pitch," but while most of the violence had been carried out against Black property, the newspaper claimed, "Negroes Precipitated Race Feeling by Appearing with Guns and Axes."[369] The situation ended in high tragedy when militiamen opened fire on the crowd outside the jail on July 6 with an eventual death toll of twelve. The story was covered at the time in newspapers across the country and the world.[370]

Racism was part and parcel of Evansville life, and to pretend otherwise is to lose an essential part of the city's past. A perfect exemplar of the racist world in which Black citizens of Evansville lived is the imagery that the *Courier* displayed on its front page in the early part of the twentieth century. From 1906 until 1960, the genius cartoonist Karl Kae Knecht was the *Courier*'s daily editorial cartoonist, and especially in that early period, his cartoons unmistakably reflected a racist worldview. Five of the first twenty-seven cartoons that he drew for the paper in 1906 involved crude and stereotypical racist depictions of Black people. He drew at least one such cartoon as late as 1937—and though these are comic drawings, the impact is extremely serious.[371] According to the historian Roger Fischer, "The genre was grandly racist: caricatures replete with grossly exaggerated lips, huge splayed feet, and kinky hair; tortured dialect imitative of minstrelsy; and situational satire that sank…low."[372] This depiction was almost literally everywhere in American culture and was sometimes referred to as "Sambo," which one historian called "an illustration of humor as a device of oppression."[373] This was the world that Black people lived with in Evansville, and as will be seen, it did not change much over the decades ahead.

Added to this is the reality that de facto racial segregation in housing was very much a fact of life for much of Evansville's history. The Howell neighborhood is a notorious example. According to Darrel Bigham, talking of the late 1920s, "members of the black community were aware of the unwritten rule that blacks did not spend the night in that community." It was, in effect, a "sundown town."[374] In 1980, Emma Gray, a Black woman, recalled her Evansville childhood: "You had to pick your time to go through Howell…because black people were not allowed in Howell, especially after dark. You had to time yourself very carefully."[375] And in 1971, Manuel Milligan recalled, "I was walking down the street over in the Howell area some years ago and some of the little kids yelled 'Hey, ain't you a [N-word]? Mamma said you were.'"[376]

Milligan's recollections are a stark reminder that racist language, and grotesque racist stereotypes, were part and parcel of life for Black people in Evansville from the beginning. Frank M. Gilbert, in one of the earliest and

One of Karl Kae Knecht's racist cartoons in the *Courier*, 1906. *UoE.*

most influential published histories of Evansville, described Black people as "ignorant, shiftless [N-words]…the offspring of the worthless [N-words]."[377] The N-word was used with monotonous regularity throughout Evansville's history. It features thousands of times in local newspapers between 1850 and today. Members of the lynch mob who were attacking the jail in 1903 called the men who were defending it and its Black prisoners "[N-word] lovers," and almost one hundred years later, the white CEO of the Evansville Housing Authority was accused of using the same word. It is perhaps telling that both the *Journal-News* in 1903 and the *Courier and Press* in 1998 chose to use dashes for other swear words but printed the N-word in full.[378] Mattie Miller, the first Black woman to teach at a white school in Evansville in 1959, encountered the word written on a classroom window.[379] Charlie Wiggins, one of the greatest Black race car drivers, was called the slur on his first day working in an Evansville garage in 1914.[380] A Black Evansville mother in 1969 had to try to explain why her son was called the word by his white best friend.[381] In 1993, as a Black *Courier* reporter sat in a housing complex parking lot, a white woman shouted, "Is that a [N-word]?"[382] Racism is an ugly and shameful part of Evansville's history that has often been conveniently lost. But to understand the city's past and, indeed, its present, the city must acknowledge and confront this part of its history. Only then can the people of Evansville, perhaps, find ways to move forward together.

With all that background, the violence that happened in 1968—an explosive year in an explosive decade—is much less surprising. There were many incidents of race-related violence in the city, and there were several racial confrontations in and around Evansville high schools. On April 15, there was an organized arson attack against the downtown Central High School, only thwarted by a witness and by police officers who broke into the school to douse the flames. Mayor Frank McDonald responded sternly, instructing police to shoot people seen handling Molotov cocktails.[383] The perpetrators turned out to be a group of Black youths who were quickly arrested. At least part of the motive, it was claimed, was racial discrimination at Central, while one report claimed that they belonged to a group called "The Black Union."[384] In October, there were clashes between Black and white students from Central; some students were injured, and some were arrested after a confrontation that took place during the visit of the pro-segregation presidential candidate George Wallace, who spoke at a rally on the courthouse steps.[385] White students later complained to the mayor, claiming, "Everyone is afraid to go where there are Negroes. We have to be with four or five others." There had been "at least one incident where Negro

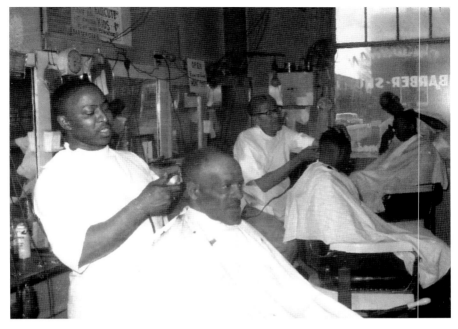

Life goes on in Black Evansville, Moorman's Barber Shop, Lincoln Avenue. *EAAM.*

youths reportedly beat up a Central student." The mayor's response was to urge them to "unite together, both Negro and white, to stop this stuff."[386] There was also sporadic trouble at Bosse High School, plainclothes police officers were deployed inside Central and that weekend's scheduled football game between Central and Bosse was canceled "at the request of the local Police Department and city officials."[387]

All this was happening just two months after the city saw a forty-eight-hour curfew when disorder erupted in the poor Black section of the city.[388] Trouble started Thursday, August 22, with Black youths throwing rocks at cars and a white youth shooting an arrow at them. A fire was set, and several buildings had their windows broken. Violence worsened Friday night into Saturday morning with businesses attacked, shots fired and some missiles thrown.[389] The city's emergency plan was activated about 2.30 a.m., with riot police deployed in large numbers close to the Club Paradise on Lincoln Avenue. Charles Schleper reported, "A policeman was wounded by a sniper and a 3-alarm fire virtually destroyed a lumber company early today to climax the second night of racial disturbances in the Lincoln-Governor area. The outbreak was the worst racial strife

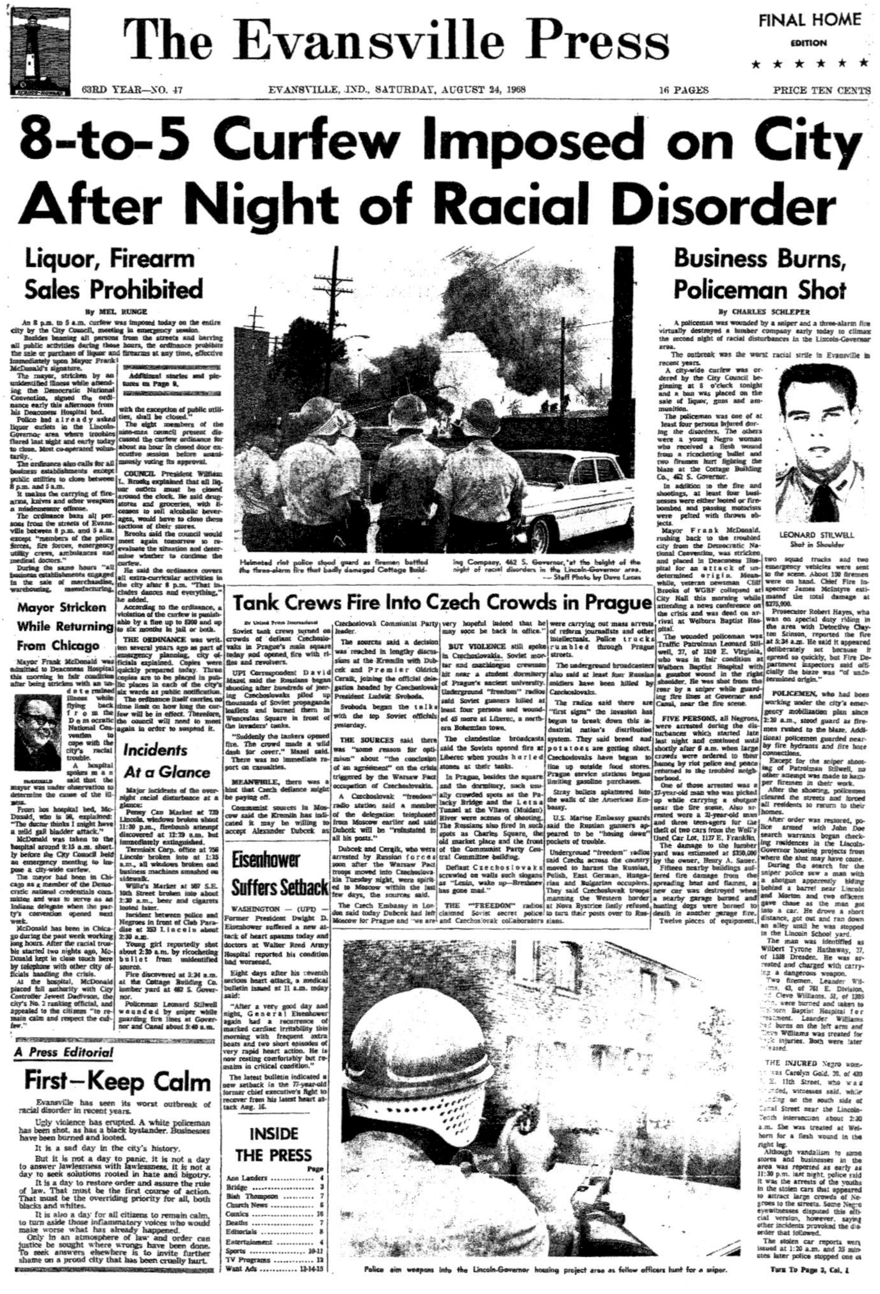

FINAL HOME EDITION

The Evansville Press

63RD YEAR—NO. 47 EVANSVILLE, IND., SATURDAY, AUGUST 24, 1968 16 PAGES PRICE TEN CENTS

8-to-5 Curfew Imposed on City After Night of Racial Disorder

Liquor, Firearm Sales Prohibited

By MEL RUNGE

An 8 p.m. to 5 a.m. curfew was imposed today on the entire city by the City Council, meeting in emergency session.

Besides banning all persons from the streets and barring all public activities during those hours, the ordinance prohibits the sale or purchase of liquor and firearms at any time, effective immediately upon Mayor Frank McDonald's signature.

The mayor, stricken by an unidentified illness while attending the Democratic National Convention, signed the ordinance early this afternoon from his Deaconess Hospital bed.

Police had already asked liquor outlets in the Lincoln-Governor area where troubles flared last night and early today to close. Most co-operated voluntarily.

The ordinance also calls for all business establishments except public utilities to close between 8 p.m. and 5 a.m.

It makes the carrying of firearms, knives and other weapons a misdemeanor offense.

The ordinance bans all persons from the streets of Evansville between 8 p.m. and 5 a.m. except "members of the police forces, fire forces, emergency utility crews, ambulances and medical doctors."

During the same hours "all business establishments engaged in the sale of merchandise, warehousing, manufacturing,

Additional stories and pictures on Page 9.

with the exception of public utilities, shall be closed."

The eight members of the nine-man council present discussed the curfew ordinance for about an hour in closed door executive session before unanimously voting its approval.

COUNCIL President William L. Brooks explained that all liquor outlets must be closed around the clock. He said drugstores and groceries, with licenses to sell alcoholic beverages, would have to close these sections of their stores.

Brooks said the council would meet again tomorrow to reevaluate the situation and determine whether to continue the curfew.

He said the ordinance covers all extra-curricular activities in the city after 8 p.m. "That includes dances and everything," he added.

According to the ordinance, a violation of the curfew is punishable by a fine up to $300 and up to six months in jail or both.

THE ORDINANCE was written several years ago as part of emergency planning, city officials explained. Copies were quickly prepared today. Three copies are to be placed in public places in each of the city's six wards as public notification.

The ordinance itself carries no time limit on how long the curfew will be in effect. Therefore, the council will need to meet again in order to suspend it.

Mayor Stricken While Returning From Chicago

Mayor Frank McDonald was admitted to Deaconess Hospital this morning in fair condition after being stricken with an undetermined illness while flying back from the Democratic National Convention to cope with the city's racial trouble.

MCDONALD

A hospital spokesman said that the mayor was under observation to determine the cause of the illness.

From his hospital bed, McDonald, who is 56, explained: "The doctor thinks I might have a mild gall bladder attack."

McDonald was taken to the hospital around 9:15 a.m. shortly before the City Council held an emergency meeting to impose a city-wide curfew.

The mayor had been in Chicago as a member of the Democratic national credentials committee and was to serve as an Indiana delegate when the party's convention opened next week.

McDonald has been in Chicago during the past week working long hours. After the racial trouble started two nights ago, McDonald kept in close touch here by telephone with other city officials handling the crisis.

At the hospital, McDonald placed full authority with City Controller Jewett Dedivson, the city's No. 2 ranking official, and appealed to the citizens "to remain calm and respect the curfew."

Incidents At a Glance

Major incidents of the overnight racial disturbance at a glance:

Penny Can Market at 729 Lincoln, windows broken about 11:30 p.m., firebomb attempt discovered at 12:29 a.m. but immediately extinguished.

Terminix Corp. office at 756 Lincoln broken into at 1:25 a.m., all windows broken and business machines smashed on sidewalk.

Willie's Market at 507 S.E. 10th Street broken into about 1:30 a.m., beer and cigarets looted later.

Incident between police and Negroes in front of Club Paradise at 253 Lincoln about 2:30 a.m.

Young girl reportedly shot about 2:30 a.m. by ricocheting bullet from unidentified source.

Fire discovered at 5:34 a.m. at the Cottage Building Co. lumber yard at 462 S. Governor.

Policeman Leonard Stilwell wounded by sniper while guarding fire lines at Governor and Canal about 5:40 a.m.

Helmeted riot police stood guard as firemen battled the three-alarm fire that badly damaged Cottage Building Company, 462 S. Governor, at the height of the night of racial disorders in the Lincoln-Governor area. — Staff Photo by Dave Lucas

Tank Crews Fire Into Czech Crowds in Prague

By United Press International

Soviet tank crews turned on crowds of defiant Czechoslovaks in Prague's main square today and opened fire with rifles and revolvers.

UPI Correspondent David Mazel said the Russians began shooting after hundreds of jeering Czechoslovaks piled up thousands of Soviet propaganda leaflets and burned them in Wenceslas Square in front of the invaders' tanks.

"Suddenly the tankers opened fire. The crowd made a wild dash for cover," Mazel said.

There was no immediate report on casualties.

MEANWHILE, there was a hint that Czech defiance might be paying off.

Communist sources in Moscow said the Kremlin has indicated it may be willing to accept Alexander Dubcek as Czechoslovak Communist Party leader.

The sources said a decision was reached in lengthy discussions at the Kremlin with Dubcek and Premier Oldrich Cernik, joining the official delegation headed by Czechoslovak President Ludvik Svoboda.

Svoboda began the talks with the top Soviet officials yesterday.

THE SOURCES said there was "some reason for optimism" about "the conclusion of an agreement" on the crisis triggered by the Warsaw Pact occupation of Czechoslovakia.

A Czechoslovak "freedom" radio station said a member of the delegation telephoned from Moscow earlier and said Dubcek will be "reinstated in all his posts."

Dubcek and Cernik, who were arrested by Russian forces soon after the Warsaw Pact troops moved into Czechoslovakia Tuesday night, were spirited to Moscow within the last few days, the sources said.

The Czech Embassy in London said today Dubcek had left Moscow for Prague and "we are very hopeful indeed that he may soon be back in office."

BUT VIOLENCE still spoke in Czechoslovakia. Soviet mortar and machinegun crewmen hit near a student dormitory of Prague's ancient university. Underground "freedom" radios said Soviet gunners killed at least four persons and wounded 45 more at Liberec, a northern Bohemian town.

The clandestine broadcasts said the Soviets opened fire at Liberec when youths hurled stones at their tanks.

In Prague, besides the square and the dormitory, such usually crowded spots as the Palacky Bridge and the Letna Tunnel at the Vltava (Moldau) River were scenes of shooting. The Russians also fired in such spots as Charles Square, the old market place and the front of the Communist Party Central Committee building.

Defiant Czechoslovaks scrawled on walls such slogans as "Lenin, wake up—Brezhnev has gone mad."

THE "FREEDOM" radios claimed Soviet secret police and Czechoslovak collaborators were carrying out mass arrests of reform journalists and other intellectuals. Police trucks rumbled through Prague streets.

The underground broadcasters also said at least four Russian soldiers have been killed by Czechoslovaks.

The radios said there are "first signs" the invasion has begun to break down this industrial nation's distribution system. They said bread and potatoes are getting short. Czechoslovaks have begun to line up outside food stores. Prague service stations began limiting gasoline purchases.

Stray bullets splattered into the walls of the American Embassy.

U.S. Marine Embassy guards said the Russian gunners appeared to be "hosing down" pockets of trouble.

Underground "freedom" radios said Czechs across the country moved to harass the Russian, Polish, East German, Hungarian and Bulgarian occupiers. They said Czechoslovak troops manning the Western border at Nova Bystrice flatly refused to turn their posts over to Russians.

Eisenhower Suffers Setback

WASHINGTON — (UPI) — Former President Dwight D. Eisenhower suffered a new attack of heart spasms today and doctors at Walter Reed Army Hospital reported his condition had worsened.

Eight days after his seventh serious heart attack, a medical bulletin issued at 11 a.m. today said:

"After a very good day and night, General Eisenhower again had a recurrence of marked cardiac irritability this morning with frequent extra beats and two short episodes of very rapid heart action. He is now resting comfortably but remains in critical condition."

The latest bulletin indicated a new setback in the 77-year-old former chief executive's fight to recover from his latest heart attack Aug. 16.

INSIDE THE PRESS

Business Burns, Policeman Shot

By CHARLES SCHLEPER

A policeman was wounded by a sniper and a three-alarm fire virtually destroyed a lumber company early today to climax the second night of racial disturbances in the Lincoln-Governor area.

The outbreak was the worst racial strife in Evansville in recent years.

A city-wide curfew was ordered by the City Council beginning at 8 o'clock tonight and a ban was placed on the sale of liquor, guns and ammunition.

The policeman was one of at least four persons injured during the disorders. The others were a young Negro woman who received a flesh wound from a ricocheting bullet and two firemen hurt fighting the blaze at the Cottage Building Co., 462 S. Governor.

In addition to the fire and shootings, at least four businesses were either looted or firebombed and passing motorists were pelted with thrown objects.

Mayor Frank McDonald, rushing back to the troubled city from the Democratic National Convention, was stricken and placed in Deaconess Hospital for an attack of undetermined origin. Meanwhile, veteran newsman Cliff Brooks of WGBF collapsed at City Hall this morning while attending a news conference on the crisis and was dead on arrival at Welborn Baptist Hospital.

The wounded policeman was Traffic Patrolman Leonard Stilwell, 27, of 1810 E. Virginia, who was in fair condition at Welborn Baptist Hospital with a gunshot wound in the right shoulder. He was shot from the rear by a sniper while guarding fire lines at Governor and Canal, near the fire scene.

FIVE PERSONS, all Negroes, were arrested during the disturbances which started late last night and continued until shortly after 6 a.m. when large crowds were ordered to their homes by riot police and peace returned to the troubled neighborhood.

One of those arrested was a 27-year-old man who was picked up while carrying a shotgun near the fire scene. Also arrested were a 21-year-old man and three teen-agers for the theft of two cars from the Well's Used Car Lot, 1127 E. Franklin.

The damage to the lumber yard was estimated at $250,000 by the owner, Henry A. Sauer.

Fifteen nearby buildings suffered fire damage from the spreading heat and flames, a new car was destroyed when a nearby garage burned and hunting dogs were burned to death in another garage fire.

Twelve pieces of equipment,

LEONARD STILWELL
Shot in Shoulder

two squad trucks and two emergency vehicles were sent to the scene. About 150 firemen were on hand. Chief Fire Inspector James McIntyre estimated the total damage at $275,000.

Prosecutor Robert Hayes, who was on special duty riding in the area with Detective Clayton Stinson, reported the fire at 5:34 a.m. He said it appeared deliberately set because it spread so quickly, but Fire Department inspectors said officially the blaze was "of undetermined origin."

POLICEMEN, who had been working under the city's emergency mobilization plan since 2:20 a.m., stood guard as firemen rushed to the blaze. Additional policemen guarded nearby fire hydrants and fire hose connections.

Except for the sniper shooting of Patrolman Stilwell, no other attempt was made to hamper firemen in their work.

After the shooting, policemen cleared the streets and forced all residents to return to their homes.

After order was restored, police armed with John Doe search warrants began checking residences in the Lincoln-Governor housing projects from where the shot may have come.

During the search for the sniper police saw a man with a shotgun apparently hiding behind a barrel near Lincoln and Morton and two officers gave chase as the man got into a car. He drove a short distance, got out and ran down an alley until he was stopped in the Lincoln School yard.

The man was identified as Wilbert Tyrone Hathaway, 27, of 1528 Dresden. He was arrested and charged with carrying a dangerous weapon.

Two firemen, Leander Williams, 43, of 761 E. Division, and Cleve Williams, 51, of 1305 [illegible], were burned and taken to Welborn Baptist Hospital for treatment. Leander Williams had burns on the left arm and Cleve Williams was treated for [illegible] injuries. Both were later released.

THE INJURED Negro woman was Carolyn Gold, 20, of 430 [illegible] E. 11th Street, who was wounded, witnesses said, while standing on the south side of Canal Street near the Lincoln-Tenth intersection about 2:30 a.m. She was treated at Welborn for a flesh wound in the right leg.

Although vandalism to some stores and businesses in the area was reported as early as 11:30 p.m. last night, police said it was the arrests of the youths in the stolen cars that appeared to attract large crowds of Negroes to the streets. Some Negro eyewitnesses disputed this official version, however, saying other incidents provoked the disorder that followed.

The stolen car reports were issued at 1:20 a.m. and 25 minutes later police stopped one of

Turn To Page 2, Col. 1

Police aim weapons into the Lincoln-Governor housing project area as fellow officers hunt for a sniper.

A Press Editorial

First—Keep Calm

Evansville has seen its worst outbreak of racial disorder in recent years.

Ugly violence has erupted. A white policeman has been shot, as has a black bystander. Businesses have been burned and looted.

It is a sad day in the city's history.

But it is not a day to panic, it is not a day to answer lawlessness with lawlessness, it is not a day to seek solutions rooted in hate and bigotry.

It is a day to restore order and assure the rule of law. That must be the first course of action. That must be the overriding priority for all, both blacks and whites.

It is also a day for all citizens to remain calm, to turn aside those inflammatory voices who would make worse what has already happened.

Only in an atmosphere of law and order can justice be sought where wrongs have been done. To seek answers elsewhere is to invite further shame on a proud city that has been cruelly hurt.

Coverage of the 1968 curfew. *EVPL*.

in Evansville in recent years." The fire caused an estimated $250,000 of damage to the lumber company on Governor Street, with the fire damaging a further fifteen buildings.[390] The city's response was to impose an 8:00 p.m. to 5:00 p.m. curfew, with a ban on alcohol and weapons sales. Police patrolled in cars with four or five officers, who were "armed to the hilt. In addition to their .38 caliber service revolvers and recent issues of chemical Mace, officers carried privately owned rifles, shotguns and automatic carbines." A combination of rainy weather and the curfew seemed to cool things down, and after forty-eight hours, the curfew was lifted.[391] The police chief, Darwin Covert, explained the disorder by saying, "There is no particular rhyme or reason. It's a spontaneous kind of thing." But the Black community had a different perspective; one young man named Otis Northington said, "It is so many things. They build up." Another echoed his words, speaking of various provocations by local white men: "It is the same old thing, and it just builds and builds."[392] The possibility of violence in the city had been signaled two years earlier when John M. Caldwell told the Housing Authority, "We are not immune to racial violence....All it would take is somebody to say, 'Let's go.'"[393] In 1968, it happened.

It happened again in the summer of 1969 following the shooting death of a young Black man named Jeffrey Taylor on Thursday, July 10. Rocks were thrown, fires were started and the police cleared the streets at 3.30 a.m. According to Taylor's friend Darrell Watkins, the death was a result of a shot from a passing car, and this version of events was what provoked the subsequent disorder. Friday night saw an escalation of the violence, with multiple fire bombings and false alarms and four people getting shot. Police were shot at by sniper fire on Canal Street, and at 10:15 p.m. the mayor declared a state of emergency and the city council imposed a curfew. By Sunday, things had calmed down, with only sporadic incidents, and the curfew was lifted; there had been 108 arrests for curfew violations.[394] Police investigated the death of Taylor vigorously, but it later emerged that Darrell Watkins was lying and his friend died from a shot accidentally discharged by Watkins himself.[395]

The fault lines remained evident into the next decade. In 1970, racial tension was so intense at Harrison High School that one radical Black publication claimed that Black students there feared for their safety: "The Black students of Harrison Highschool [sic], have undergone intimidation, threats, and harassment, apparently because of prejudices from white students....It was reported that older men, apparently white parents, have been harassing Black students [and] calling them names, etc., coming to

Life In Evansville's Negro Ghetto

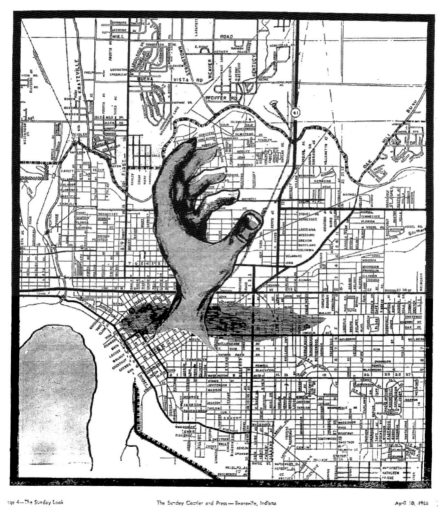

This staggering image accompanied a 1966 *SCP* story about life and death in Baptistown. The headline shown here actually spread over two pages. *EVPL/EEAM.*

pick up their children, carrying with them hammers, expecting trouble which in itself is aggravating."[396] At Reitz, tension built over the course of 1971, with a late October fight over a bag of candy, in which a white student got cut by a box-cutter, exacerbating the tensions.[397] Tension grew as rumors flew. Black students at Reitz—who made up the lowest proportion of any city high school at just 5 percent of the student body—felt unheard and unrepresented. There was a brief picket of the school by some Black students, and then trouble erupted again on November 8, with twenty Black students being arrested at the school. There were fights including both male and female students.[398] The student council responded with a letter that said, "We feel that in the past Reitz has not been the school to some that it should have been but we as individuals would sincerely like to work to assure each student that he is a part of Reitz High School."[399]

Things calmed down on the West Side, but on the other side of town, simmering racial tension once again came to the surface in an outburst of deadly violence that began in the summer of 1973 and continued into 1974. In June, days of disorder and violence around Lincoln and Governor followed the likely racist murder of Jeffrey Wayne Thomas. He was a Black man from Evansville, murdered in Posey County by a white man. Among those who appealed for calm was Thomas's brother Willie Thomas IV, a longtime community organizer and someone who had been identified two years earlier by the FBI covert surveillance program known as COINTELPRO as a leader of the Black Panther Party in Evansville. His request that "my brothers and sisters in the area...stay cool" was successful, and calm was restored.[400] Four months later, at about 3:30 a.m. on October 11, a white rookie police officer named John Zirkelbach shot and killed a Black youth, seventeen-year-old Walter Peaches, who was fleeing the scene of a burglary at the Outta Sight Lounge on Canal Street. The case aroused considerable controversy in the Black community, especially when an all-white grand jury found no reason to indict the police officer, and an Evansville police trial board also concluded a few days later that he had done nothing wrong. The youth's mother filed suit against the city and Officer Zirkelbach, with the case dragging on through the courts for years. In 1979, the Indiana Court of Appeals found in favor of the defendants, and the U.S. Supreme Court, without comment, refused to review the case in January 1980.[401] The death of Walter Peaches left the city simmering, and tension continued as 1974 dawned.

There were several weeks of sporadic violence that saw fights, threats and shootings culminating on April 27, when a Black man, James R. Ellis, was shot and killed by the white manager of the Belmont Tavern on SE Eighth Street. The Black community, which thought negatively of the Belmont already, were then further enraged when Ellis's accused killer was allowed to walk free on bond of $1,000, despite being charged with murder. There

Police stand between groups of Black and white students during unrest outside Central High School, November 1975. *USI.*

followed an increase in violence: the Belmont was firebombed; cars were fired on at the intersections of Eighth and Canal and Riverside and Adams; and on May 4, a white man, David O'Keefe, was shot and wounded in his car while his three-year-old child sat on the front seat beside him. The previous day, a white couple, Donald and Peggy Hamilton, were both shot by a Black assailant while their vehicle was stopped at a red light at Lincoln and Governor. Mrs. Hamilton was shot in the head and seriously injured. Gary Tyrone Seay, seventeen, was charged and ultimately convicted of this attack; in court it was alleged that he had said that he "had been thinking about his friend, Walter Peaches."[402] Tensions continued for another five days, and on May 7, a Black youth named Keith Foreman was shot from inside a passing pickup truck as he stood outside a house on East Blackford Avenue; he died hours later in hospital. Mayor Russell Lloyd, who had cut short a trip to rush back to the city, announced that all police leave was canceled and police officers were to work twelve-hour shifts; the Vanderburgh County Sheriff's Department stood on alert. There were isolated incidents, including restroom wastebaskets being set on fire at Bosse High School as students reacted to their former classmate Foreman's murder. The U.S. Community Relations Service was concerned enough to dispatch two of its community relations specialists down from Chicago to Evansville on May 8.[403] In a forceful editorial, the *Press* declared,

> *Six nighttime shootings in less than a week have left one black teenager dead, three whites wounded—one woman still in critical condition—and a City made fearful. Accounts by witnesses and victims are sketchy, but in every case they indicate racial attacks....It is woefully apparent that there is little real understanding between the races here and even less active effort to create it. With a black population of 7 per cent, it is astonishing that Evansville still must refer to one of its neighborhoods by the modish euphemism of "inner city."*[404]

The summer of 1974 was fairly peaceful, but on September 19, several people were injured and five Black youths were arrested following violence at the Harrison-North football game. The following day, trouble continued at Harrison High School when "a morning filled with incidents such as tripping, name-calling and food-throwing in the cafeteria came to a head." Groups of Black and white students gathered in the parking lots, where there were scuffles and arrests, and the school closed at 11:10 a.m.[405] It reopened on Monday morning but with rules against gatherings between classes and with both parents and police present. A group of Black leaders met with the mayor, one of whom, Bobby Ogburn, said that Black people were "sick and tired of being pushed around," while the group also "protested alleged police brutality to Negro students and complained that uniformed officers took off their badges Friday making identification for purposes of filing complaints difficult."[406] Things quietened down, but no sooner had

Harrison returned to normality than Bosse High School erupted in further "racial unrest." Over three hundred students left school and did not return on Thursday, September 26; the next day, police were called to break up gatherings of students, and Principal Paul Jennings said that he would ask parents to accompany their children to school on Monday "in an effort to prevent further incidents there."[407] He was quoted in the *Press* saying, "I don't think anybody knows the solution. We don't even know the reason for the problem." Journalist Dale McConnaughay tried to be balanced when he suggested, "Although the blame for yesterday's trouble was directed largely at white students, the history of racial antagonisms at Bosse is a long one with both sides contributing their fair share of fuel to the fire." Jennings acknowledged that the students called each other's racial group the N-word and "Honky" but said that such language only became common at times of "strain" like the past few days.[408] The editor of the *Press*, Michael Grehl, offered an eloquent and depressing editorial comment on September 28 when he said, "We are watching groups of white kids and black kids glaring at each other across the school ground. Or worse. With police on full alert… it is catastrophic to see them fall into the same old traps over race and surrender to the same old fears."[409] There was further trouble at Central High School just over a year later—ten students were eventually arrested after a racial confrontation in the school parking lot.[410]

The situation was certainly imperfect, but the very fact that Black and white were in class together was much better than the way things had been for decades. It had taken enormous, often grudging, efforts to get Evansville to a situation where Black and white students attended the same schools, and it is to this effort that we now turn. The story of Evansville's school integration journey is a fascinating one and one that reflects many of the key issues of American society at the time. It is also important to remember that this is a complex and multifaceted issue; although desegregation of public schools was a step forward for the city of Evansville, it was a process that also had negative repercussions for the Black community. The community lost cohesion and arguably a significant component of its identity as students were divided up between previously all-white schools where they often felt alienated and unwelcome. While this is mostly a discussion of K–12 education, it is worth mentioning that Evansville College admitted its first Black student in 1934 when Lincoln High School's Zerah Carter enrolled; this was the year before the NAACP launched its first successful legal challenge to separate college education in the *Murray v. Pearson* case. It was said that the Evansville College president Earl Harper asked for someone who would "see

Black Evansville. Governor Street runs top to bottom, and bottom right is the corner of Lincoln Gardens. The area of rubble towards the middle is where the Erie Homes were to be built. *USI.*

and not see" and "hear and not hear" the racism that they were expected to encounter. Carter's teachers at Lincoln High School warned her that she would encounter "unpleasant situations" and that she was effectively a "test case."[411] Despite everything, Carter graduated in 1938, followed by Vera Lee Shane and Gertie Gracey one year later.[412]

With K–12 education, before 1949, individual Indiana school boards could decide for themselves the extent of segregation that they practiced. With the passage that year of the Indiana Educational Nonsegregation Law, however, it was now the policy of the state to "abolish, eliminate and prohibit segregated and separate schools or school districts on the basis of race, creed or color."[413] This, it should be noted with pride by all Hoosiers, was five years before *Brown v. Board of Education*. The Evansville-Vanderburgh School Corporation (EVSC), had not only maintained a segregated system, wrote U.S. District Judge S. Hugh Dillon in a 1972 judgment, "but it cooperated in maintaining all white public schools in communities outside the borders of Vanderburgh County by accepting enforced transfers of Negro pupils from such places as Boonville and Yankeetown, in Warrick County, and Rockport, in Spencer County, to its all black schools located in central Evansville."[414]

The EVSC complied with the new law in a half-hearted manner; in the words of journalist Nancy Hutchinson, "In September of 1949, the double [segregated] system of school districting remained in effect, but students in kindergarten, first and ninth grades were given the choice of enrolling in either the black or white school in their districts." The immediate impact was miniscule: seven Black students enrolled at both Culver and Wheeler, four at Delaware and just one at Central.[415] At Culver, the four Black children in kindergarten and the three first graders were almost instantly enough to provoke a group of white parents to petition the school board for their removal, citing "ill feeling" and "growing friction" at the school, which they blamed on the presence of the Black children.[416] A woman named Specht told the school board, "It's degrading to send my children to school with Negroes."[417] The school board refused to take action on this complaint, but its self-described "middle of the road" policy was in fact far from radical and basically maintained a mostly segregated system.[418] Further protests followed when Harwood School was integrated in 1954; white parents picketed with signs that said, "You have your school—We have ours," "Go Back to Your Own Schools" and "We Are Against Insegration [*sic*]." Margaret Repperdam, one of the picketers, said, "I don't want my child to go to school with Negro children," while another added, "I didn't go to school with Negroes, so why should my children?"[419] A Black man who was watching, Frank Carter, uttered the memorable line, "There is no place for ignorance in society in the USA. And I've seen the ignorantest [*sic*] people this morning I've ever seen in my life."[420]

Two events in Washington, DC, however, were to force the EVSC's timid hand. The second Supreme Court decision on school segregation, *Brown v. Board of Education II* of 1955, clarified that school desegregation had to happen "with all deliberate speed," and the 1964 Civil Rights Act led to the Department of Health, Education and Welfare (HEW) targeting school districts that were practicing segregation.[421] In 1966, the EVSC went forward with a voluntary transfer plan, followed by a racial balance redistricting plan in 1970 that involved "five pie-shaped districts, with each cutting into the central part of the city." The redistricting was intended to balance the high schools in terms of numbers, race, and socioeconomic status.[422] In the eyes of the Office of Civil Rights at HEW, however, the EVSC had not moved far enough, announcing in September 1971 that the EVSC was not in compliance with the Civil Rights Act of 1964. The main problem in their view was Lincoln School, whose 99.8 percent Black enrollment made it in HEW's words "clearly a vestige of the dual system."[423] The EVSC response

The Evansville Press

THURSDAY, DEC. 18, 1969

PAGE 25

Boundaries revised for racial balance

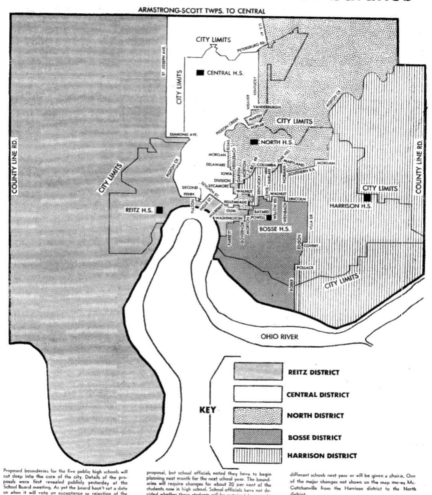

The "pie-shaped" plan for Evansville school desegregation, 1969. *EVPL.*

was a plan to integrate the elementary schools; they decided to close three schools, initiate a "pupil exchange" involving almost three thousand students at four inner-city schools and fully integrate teaching staff across the school system. The plan was immediately strongly opposed by critics on both sides who saw it either as too little or as too much.[424] HEW approved the plan, contingent on five stipulated areas of further action, in February 1972, but due to a subsequent change of personnel on the school board and intense protests that included the picketing of school board members' homes, the board changed course and reverted to the earlier, unadjusted plan.

The result was an expedited lawsuit that was heard that summer in U.S. District Court in Indianapolis.[425] On Friday, August 11, before a packed courtroom, Judge Dillin found for the plaintiffs and ordered the EVSC to reinstate its HEW-approved desegregation plan, stating that in Evansville "all deliberate speed has run out." Before the suit was formally dismissed, school board officials had to sign documents inside the courtroom signaling their intent to reestablish the original integration plan, and the board was placed under court jurisdiction, meaning that all future plans would have to meet the court's approval.[426] The anti-integration forces were enraged and vowed to fight on—"I'm absolutely not going to comply," declared a man named Curtis Montgomery. "The Negro has made me a racist."[427] His wife and others began to organize a white-only "freedom school" that was tentatively scheduled to open in September but never materialized. The "freedom school" was an echo of a tactic that had happened in many parts of the South after *Brown v. Board*.[428] In Evansville, it was almost definitely motivated by racism but was publicly justified by concerns that their white children would be attending Lincoln school in what they considered an unsafe (Black) neighborhood: "It's even unsafe for their own kind," said Mrs. Montgomery. "We know the kinds of things that go on down there; the dope, the sex, and everything else….[Black people] are really slaves again if they bow to [court-ordered busing]." This, too, was rhetoric that was seen in many parts of the country.[429] Despite these loud voices, this part of the battle was largely over. Talmadge Vick, a Black teacher and one of those responsible for the lawsuit, said, "It was a very momentous decision that will lay the groundwork for years to come."[430] The plan was far from perfect, and there would be many more bumps on the road; a further plan was implemented in 1974. As has been seen, integration did not mean that peace would reign in the schools. But for Evansville, a city with much racism in its history, the battle for school desegregation had been, to a significant extent, won.

Willie Effie Thomas. *EC.*

An earlier battle, just as momentous, was over the desegregation of public facilities in the city. On Monday, March 26, 1956, a Black couple, Reverend and Mrs. Arthur Lee Jelks, bought their tickets for the popular film noir *The Phenix City Story* and attempted to enter the Columbia Theater on Fulton Avenue. According to Reverend Jelks, they were stopped at the door and told, "I am sure some mistake has been made. Negroes have never come in here. We would have to get the police to come in with you so as to protect your safety." The police duly arrived, and Reverend Jelks was able to sit in his seat, but he said, "We were very much hurt over the incident. Mrs. Jelks' nerves were very much upset." He later reflected, "I have been in Evansville only five months and I didn't come here to make trouble. I didn't seek entrance to that theater to make trouble. I was under the impression that theaters were open to all races, as required by law."[431]

Jelks has been said to be "in the forefront of breaking up segregation"[432] in Evansville, but he in turn was inheriting a tradition of defiance that had already been established in the city. Reverend W.D. Shannon, pastor (as Jelks would later be) of the Alexander African Methodist Episcopal Church, helped form the first chapter of the NAACP in Evansville in 1915, trying and failing to prevent the racist blockbuster *Birth of a Nation* from playing in a local theater; the president was William Best, and the secretary was Sallie Stewart.[433] In 1939 and 1940, the NAACP campaigned to allow Black students into the newly opened Mechanic Arts School, from which they were excluded.[434] Another giant in the movement was Willie Effie Thomas, who said that she moved to Evansville in the 1940s "because of the segregation in the South. But then I found as much here." Activist Solomon Stevenson recalled, "Blacks were not accepted in many, I don't know of any, eating places at that time. Downtown they sat in segregated areas. In the theaters, it was the balcony. They did not use the Central Library."[435] Longtime Lincoln High School teacher Alfred Porter's memories were similar: "The wife went in Woolworth's and asked for a drink of water, she had to go back to [ask] the manager if she could give a little child a drink of water. And as for eating uptown, forget it. Theaters, you sat upstairs behind the wide aisle. They took out a row of seats and

The Cherry Street Library, for Black patrons only. *EVPL.*

you sat there. Or at one theater you went in a side door. You bought your tickets here and went around the side door to upstairs."[436] Anita Wisdom said much the same—"You went to the show, you had a certain section. I know up here at the Majestic you used to have to go in the side and way up in the balcony. And at the Loew's Victory, you walked back 18 rows before you [could] take a seat—that was in the second balcony."[437]

In 1959, the local NAACP president, Charles H. King, claimed that there were eighteen downtown Evansville businesses that refused to serve Black people.[438] Thomas too experienced all this—she said that she sat down to have a Coke at a five-and-ten store (probably Woolworth's) downtown, but when she returned the waitress told her, "I can't serve you. The manager said I'm not supposed to." Thomas responded by getting people together to stage a sit-in and then organized "stand-ups" in a theater where Blacks were similarly restricted. Alfred Porter remembered her as "about the most active. She led the sit-ins…at theaters and eating places," while another activist described her as "one person that was very dominant…in the NAACP… [who] began to test many of these places that were discriminating against

Negroes."[439] Charles H. King was arrested in February 1959 and charged with disorderly conduct after being refused a shoeshine at Emory's Barber Shop with the alleged words, "We don't give colored people shines in this shop." Represented by attorney Sydney Berger, his case was dismissed three days later by the prosecutor O.H. Roberts on the grounds that it was not in the public interest and that a court was "not an appropriate forum for resolving complex questions concerning integration in public places with the attendant sociological problems."[440] King went on to campaign against minstrel shows in Evansville and criticize local businesses for their failure to hire Black employees—in 1959 he singled out Mead Johnson (zero Black employees), Deaconess Hospital (one) and Welborn Hospital (four). He would also condemn labor unions, the Welfare Department, the police department and the school board for their discriminatory employment practices.[441] Two other Black ministers, Major Alston and W.R. Brown, were also pioneers beside King in the struggle, entering local businesses that barred Black people and asking to be served. Alston recalled,

> *During that time, there were three Negro preachers* [King, Brown and Alston] *in Evansville* [who] *put forth tremendous efforts to try to cause some of the places to open up. A lot of people today don't know this now.…We would do that; we would go to these places.…I remember on one occasion, Brown and I went out to a barbecue place, Mac's, and they didn't accommodate or serve Negroes there. I said to the lady, "I'm a minister here. Would it be alright if sometime I would bring my friends out, four or five or more? Would we be permitted here, to eat here?" She wouldn't even say, "Hi."…There's no way for you to imagine the plight of the black man in America, going way back, without being black.*[442]

Alston, King and Brown, alongside Reverend Bransford Utley, all attended the March on Washington in 1963.[443]

It is worth noting briefly that Evansville people also influenced the civil rights movement in other places; Evansville activist Anthony Brooks Sr. was the leader of early 1960s sit-ins in Henderson, Kentucky, where he was a pastor of Seventh Street Baptist Church. Evansville speakers and lawyers were part of the Henderson sit-ins too. According to Brooks's lifelong friend Ron Sheffer, "He led the civil rights movement in Henderson. Anthony led the fight to integrate Henderson's restaurants." He also participated in the civil rights struggle in Frankfort and Louisville, marching in both places with Martin Luther King Jr.[444] Charles H. King was not an Evansville native but

Lincoln Gardens, with Miller Pool bottom right. The diagonal street is Canal. *USI.*

had a large impact both in the city and nationwide. He participated in the civil rights movement in Selma, Alabama, in 1965. Pastor of Liberty Baptist Church from 1956 to 1966, Brooks left Evansville for Gary, Indiana, where he served on the Human Relations Commission, and he later participated as a race relations analyst on the highly influential National Advisory Commission on Civil Disorders, known as the Kerner Commission.[445] In 1973, he founded the Urban Crisis Center in Atlanta and rose to prominence as a national expert on race relations and often led what his *New York Times* obituary called "boot camp-style seminars to help both whites and blacks change their racial attitudes."[446]

A further challenge to Evansville's racial status quo came in 1956, when the segregation of public swimming pools was challenged. At that time, there were four city pools (Artes, East Side, Garvin and Howell Park) that were exclusively for white swimmers and just one (Miller, on Governor Street) that was for Black patrons only. This segregation was common across much of the country, as, according to the historian Victoria W. Wolcott, "swimming pools and beaches were among the most segregated and fought over public spaces in the North and South."[447] White people across the country feared that they would catch diseases by sharing a pool with Black swimmers, wrote the historian Jeff Wiltse, and he cited a white woman in Marion, Indiana, who explained that whites did not want to swim with Blacks because they "didn't want to be polluted by their 'blackness.'" The challenge to segregated pools was similarly nationwide in scope.[448] In Evansville in June 1956, Reverend G. Sims Rivers, a Black member of the Recreation Commission, requested that they consider the integration of one of the pools, Artes, due to the large number of Black families that lived close to it in the Mill Terrace housing project. The very existence of Mill Terrace as a large area of Black housing far from Baptistown was a product of racial segregation—as mentioned earlier, it was established as a wartime federal housing project for Black tenants who were excluded from the other five federal housing projects in Evansville. The commission's response is revealing; they agreed to study the issue but were reluctant to take decisive action because they feared "incidents or trouble" if the pool was integrated "without the community being ready for it." They also pointed out that there had been more "deep concern or antagonism in the field of integrated swimming" than any other.[449] Again, this timidity in the face of concern over white reaction was a common perspective throughout the country.

Two days later, Arthur Jelks, part of a group called the Interdenominational Civic Committee (ICC), took direct action. Jelks and some other Black ministers led a group of Black children to Artes pool, where they were "politely" denied entry by the head lifeguard. There was a brief blockade of the pool, and then the Black group left.[450] After some discussion with

Segregated swimming at the Artes Pool, late 1940s. *WL.*

The Evansville Press

Served by United Press, Associated Press, Scripps-Howard Leased Wire, NEA Service, Science Service, United Press Telephoto and Newspictures

FIFTIETH YEAR, NO. 296   EVANSVILLE, INDIANA, MONDAY, JUNE 11, 1956

ı Grim nted ustee

rm Left
'he Death
ilkinson

'im, a Dem-
tor of the
unty Civil
zation, to-
ed Knight
: to fill the
of Repub-
inson, who
night.

nmissioners
intment at
eeting this

sioner Charles
a motion to
while Republi-
Henry Fitz-
Paul Wilkin-
ustee.
ident Wilfred
ocrat, voted
im.

iid he felt a
ave been ap-
ired term of

Race Dispute Halts Pool Registration

Registration for swimming at Artes Pool was stopped for about half an hour this morning when a group of Negro ministers protested the Recreation Commission's policy of restricting swimming there to white children. Listening to the protests, in center of group, is Morris Riley, supervisor of the city pools.

LATE NEWS
ᴮᵁᴸᴸᴱᵀᴵᴺᴳ   **Salk Says Vaccine**

Artes Pool Registration Bars Negroes

Suit Threatened
To Shut Down
Disputed Facility

Negro children today were prevented from registering for swimming instructions at Artes Pool.

As a result, the Rev. Arthur
Jelks, pastor of the Alexander
A.M.E. Church, Fifth and Walnut
streets, said a court suit would be
filed to keep the city from opening the pool at Fifth Avenue and
Keller Street.

"We're going to meet at a certain church to discuss what further steps should be taken," he
said as he and several other
Negro ministers left the pool
grounds.

The ministers, as well as several Negro adults, stopped the
registration of children shortly
after 9 a.m.—after three or four
white children had entered the
bath house to register. Registration of the white children began
again about 9:40 a.m.

No swimming was scheduled for
any of the five public pools in
the city this morning, but open
swimming—was set for 1 p.m. No
registration incidents were re-

Me Fir To

Gilbert S(
New Presi

By ED KLI

Employes of (
ker Steel Corpo
bought the com

Previously,
been minority s
today that the
quired a contr
est.

The announceme
retirement from b
Dr. Roderick Mar
sota, Fla., who h
dent of the 75-yea
old.

It was revealed [
had several oppor

The campaign to desegregate the city swimming pools, 1956. *EVPL*

city officials and considering their options, the ICC and the NAACP decided to file suit on behalf of thirty-three Black children against the City of Evansville and various public officials. The suit was filed on June 26 by local attorney Sydney Berger and two Indianapolis lawyers.[451] Within three days, the city announced that segregation in all pools and public recreation areas would end immediately, and by Sunday, July 1, integrated swimming was happening at Garvin pool, where "there was no disturbance and many of the white children seemed unaware of the Negro youngsters. At the deep end of the pool, several Negro boys and a number of white boys dived from the diving board, waiting in an orderly line for their turns at the board." At Artes pool, however, there was no swimming by either Black or white; someone had thrown broken glass into the pool the night before. Morris Riley, municipal pools supervisor, said there "was no way of knowing who threw the glass in the pool."[452] On July 2, the pool was cleared and open, with about twenty Black children swimming; the federal suit was dropped a day later, and the ICC and the NAACP released a statement that concluded,

It is especially timely on this approaching anniversary of the signing of our Declaration of Independence to note that the children of Evansville who are now swimming and playing and going to school together will grow up to work together to carry out the truth proclaimed in the Declaration of Independence: "that all men are created equal that they are endowed by their creator with certain inalienable rights; that among these, are life, liberty, and the pursuit of happiness."[453]

One more hurdle had been crossed. Another huge hurdle remained.

As has been discussed already, Evansville had always been a deeply segregated city in terms of housing, and the final area to be discussed in this chapter is the struggle for equality in housing and specifically the struggle for an open housing ordinance in the city. Local civil rights activist Solomon Stevenson traced the struggle all the way back to May 1916, when the New York social reformer Lawrence Veiller spoke to an Evansville audience that included Benjamin Bosse and Albion Fellows Bacon.[454] But the modern push had begun in earnest in 1964, when several members of the mayor's Human Relations Commission (HRC) began discussing such an ordinance. The constitutional validity was questioned, however, and some members worried about the controversy that would be created.[455] Over the next couple of years, open housing ordinances appeared in towns and cities all over the country, and usually stirred deep controversy—in fact, in 1967, activists from Evansville were traveling to Milwaukee, Wisconsin, to march in support of the contentious measure there. One of them was Ray Anderson, leader of Evansville's Redevelopment Commission, who said, "The whole non-violent movement is on the line there."[456] By 1968, five Indiana cities had open housing ordinances: Indianapolis, Hammond, Gary, East Chicago and Bloomington.

By early 1968, the topic was dominating discussion at the Evansville chapter of the NAACP, and President Clark Johnson said that although there was a limited state law that forbade discrimination in housing, "we have to have the law right here." Wayne Collins, speaking at a February meeting, declared, "The only way to get a strong ordinance is with a city ordinance....I do not advocate militancy, but adequate legal and moral pressure can be brought to bear to create an effective housing ordinance."[457] Momentum continued to build through the spring, but

Black housing on Governor Street, 1952. EAAM.

local politicians moved slowly, citing the existence of the state law as their reason for inaction. In early February, the city council did pass a resolution supporting the existing state law—a gesture that was on the one hand redundant, as pointed out by David Koehler, but on the other hand was a powerful symbolic step. John M. Caldwell, representative of the Fourth Ward and first Black person elected to city office, spoke eloquently for the latter perspective:

I think all of us who read the signs of the times, correctly, are aware that we are in a race with catastrophe. It is obvious that we stand today at the crossroads of history. If we take the wrong path that will lead us to bitter confrontation, more shameful division, and bequeath to the next generations social chaos. Fellow Councilmen, I urge you to pass this resolution as a positive step in the direction toward equality for all.[458]

Throughout all this, the HRC struggled over how to proceed and whether or not they should be the ones to draft an open housing ordinance. This was symbolized in late February 1968, when they passed a resolution merely endorsing the city council's endorsement of the existing state law and "calling for action in changing the state statute to be more effective and to enforce the statute conscientiously." Ray Anderson, co-chair of the HRC's steering committee, said that they would also "attempt to draft a local open housing ordinance...and present it to the city council for adoption."[459] A major blockage was that the City Attorney Robert Matthews repeatedly offered his legal opinion that Indiana cities could not adopt housing ordinances because the state Civil Rights Act took precedence. Nevertheless, by late summer both the NAACP and the HRC were working on open housing ordinances that they hoped would satisfy Matthews, who could prevent anything even getting before the city council.[460] Then two important things happened in quick succession. First, a group called the Steering Committee for Black Community Action, chaired by the Reverend Robert L. Saunders and acting in response to the violence and the curfew of August, presented a nine-point list of grievances and demands to the city council; one of these demands was for an open housing ordinance.[461] And second, in early September Matthews changed his position in response to an Indiana Supreme Court case related to the open housing ordinance in the city of Gary; in fact, Matthew's changed position rested on one dissenting justice who argued that the amended Indiana Civil Rights Act did indeed give cities the right to enact open housing ordinances.[462] The city's legal staff worked long hours preparing an ordinance, and it was finally presented to the city council on Monday September 23.[463] Closely based on the existing state law, it provided much that advocates wanted but had two large flaws: it exempted "owner-occupied housing of less than four units" and had no local enforcement power. Over the following days, many disappointed activists urged that it be strengthened, and at a public hearing on October 2, "a young Negro stood before the City Council and ripped the proposed ordinance in half to demonstrate what he thought of it."[464]

A Black tenement on Canal Street, demolished in 1957, Liberty Baptist Church visible in background. *WL.*

Through October, pressure mounted to strengthen the ordinance; a delegation of Protestant ministers and Catholic priests lobbied at city hall for these changes, and Mayor Frank McDonald asked the Evansville Bar Association to set up a five-person committee to study the legality of

John M. Caldwell and Sydney Berger. *EAAM/WL.*

giving the ordinance local enforcement powers. The committee, all past presidents of the bar association, crucially included the renowned civil rights activist Sydney Berger.[465] The Indiana Conference of the NAACP sent telegrams to some of the key decision-makers reminding them that "crucial times dictate immediate action," while these same decision makers also received a 400-signature petition, mostly from people who lived in the Lincoln-Governor neighborhood.[466] The bar association committee informed the council of their decision on Saturday November 16—they had split 3–2 in favor of the legality of such an ordinance, which allowed the council to proceed. The council met for four hours in private that day to finalize the wording, and finally, on November 18, the city council unanimously passed the strengthened ordinance, with local enforcement and with no exceptions. An overflowing crowd of around 250 gave the decision a standing ovation.

A wonderful photograph accompanies the front-page story in the *Press*, showing joyful supporters—Black and white, male and female, old and young—celebrating the moment. The caption captures the event: "A standing-room-only crowd that spilled into City Hall corridors cheered last night as the Evansville City Council passed a tough, sweeping open housing ordinance in a lightning stroke." The picture showed prominent local civil rights activists, including Reverend Major Alston, Ira Neal and Sadelle Berger. Civil rights activist Talmadge Vick called open housing "a right most

A joyful image marks the passage of the open housing ordinance, 1968. *EVPL.*

Americans take for granted," while George Chester said that Black people had been tied to the ghettos by an "imaginary iron band." John M. Caldwell, who had said that an open housing ordinance was a major reason why he ran for election, referred to its passage as "the highlight of my political career."[467] Another of the key figures was Zachariah Buckner, who organized both Black and white support for the measure all over town; according to journalist Edna Folz, "Few of his friends realized that the organized efforts of 'moderate' Negroes to push for an open housing ordinance in Evansville in 1968, was born in the Buckner living room. Mr Buckner felt this was a concern of all, and the older and established Negroes should show their support of the younger ones who had been carrying the ball in this fight."[468]

The year 1968 was a traumatic one all over the United States, of course, and it had certainly been so in Evansville. Dr. Martin Luther King Jr. and Senator Robert Kennedy had been assassinated, and cities had burned from Washington, DC, to Evansville. But 1968 also saw the passage of the federal Fair Housing Bill (technically Title VIII of the 1968 Civil Rights Act) in April and the City of Evansville open housing ordinance in November.[469] Much was lost that year, but much was also gained; the Evansville ordinance was an enormous, hard-won step forward. In November 2018, the Evansville City Council marked the fiftieth anniversary of the ordinance by passing a resolution to "honor and memorialize this important milestone." They did not, however, ignore reality:

> *While the City Council welcomes this opportunity to acknowledge that there have been gains made to end racial segregation in the past 50 years, there is still considerable work to do to achieve the goals of the spirit of the Open Housing Movement and fair housing laws.*[470]

As the theologian Jim Wallis wrote, "The geography of race still separates most black Americans from most white Americans." The Promised Land, as ever, remains our hoped-for destination rather than our currently existing experience.[471]

CONCLUSION

The interest in historical preservation is more than just the buildings; it ultimately involves our whole cultural heritage. It's a way of recycling the past. Buildings are just the physical reminders of our past.[472]

These words of historian Darrel Bigham are a powerful reminder of how interlinked the various aspects of the past are and how connected the past is to the present. In Evansville, as has been said, much of the past has been lost and much of that is not only gone forever but also took many other things with it. And yet this story, which could have been a sad cavalcade of lost history, is actually the opposite. It is in fact as much a story of what has been preserved as one of what has been lost.

Clearly, much of chapter 3 discusses projects that involved the demolition of existing structures, some of which were much lamented almost as soon as they were gone. Some of the structures that replaced them were unheralded at the time and have never enjoyed much acclaim. But that moment was also the turning point, as people in Evansville realized that things could and should be done in a different way. In April 1972, in the very middle of the most intense period of "creative destruction" in the city's history, the *Press* offered this editorial:

> *A growing number of thoughtful people are coming to the conclusion that tearing down buildings is not a panacea for what plagues the American city. Rather, they are asking, isn't it time to devote more effort*

toward preserving what is historically valuable in our cities. This train of thought, which is gaining converts across the nation, is now happily taking root in Evansville.[473]

The occasion for this observation was the visit to Evansville of Indiana University's Committee on Historic Preservation and the proposal that the city get its own historic preservation committee. Eventually, after a long struggle, the city would get its historic preservation infrastructure, and a great deal of the physical past of Evansville that has been preserved is because of this.[474] The year 1972 was also when the Wesselman Park Nature Center Society was founded to protect Wesselman Woods, the single largest tract of old-growth forest inside any city in the United States. The woods had faced the same potential fate as Angel Mounds, since the Allen consulting firm, which suggested a golf course there, also proposed an eighteen-hole golf course that would have destroyed a third of the virgin forest. This idea was, however, "smothered," and Wesselman Woods remains one of the city's jewels today; it is an active and educational celebration of the city's ancient past.[475]

One of the many important figures in protecting Evansville's physical heritage was Alexander L. Leich, who played a central role in the preservation of the Old Court House and who Darrel Bigham described as "one of the city's earliest and most devoted champions of historic preservation."[476] Randall Shepard, Evansville native and chief justice of the Indiana Supreme Court, and his wife, Amy McDonell—called "the dynamic duo of preservation" in Evansville—were another two who performed vital work in preserving Evansville's physical past.[477] One name, however, stands out above all others—Joan Marchand. She was the city's historic preservation specialist in the Department of Metropolitan Development for ten years, and starting in 1978, she threw herself into that task. An excellent researcher and writer, she produced several publications and worked tirelessly to get five Evansville neighborhoods and eighty-five individual buildings onto the National Register of Historic Places. Early on, she worked at Angel Mounds, and she said that she used that training in her later position—"I used the analytical skills I learned in archaeology to help me investigate old buildings. I took to it like a duck to water." Marchand's first career was as a teacher, and she never stopped educating people—bureaucrats, homeowners and the countless people who were fascinated by her walking tours of historic areas or by her printed guides. "I know of several instances," said one of her admirers, "where Joan would tell the history of a badly deteriorated building to a potential owner and the aliveness of the history would help tip the scale on interesting that person to commit to the rehabilitation of the structure."[478] When Marchand died, one of her successors, Dennis Au, paid her a beautiful tribute. Describing her as a lost landmark, he observed that West Africans compare the loss of a knowledgeable and wise person to a library burning:

> *I felt, yes, indeed, because she had so much knowledge of this town and its architecture, a library had burned. But I'm happy to say the library didn't entirely burn. Joan Marchand in her lifetime compiled a tremendous personal library and archive. It's extremely well organized. It's a fantastic resource, an ongoing resource for the future.*[479]

Of Evansville's old buildings, Marchand once said, "They're an open-air classroom. They tell us something about what this old town looked like at one time." Without Joan Marchand, much of that classroom could have been lost.[480] And because of what she left behind, the classroom, and the library, are still open.

There has also been the vital work done by historians and archivists to ensure that the story of Evansville's past did not get lost. Building on the work of early historians Joseph P. Elliot and Frank M. Gilbert, twentieth-century historians James Morlock, Ed Klingler, Kenneth McCutchan, Harold Morgan and Robert Patry all made vital contributions, producing historical accounts that are accurate, insightful and well-written. McCutchan's history was elegantly updated by two men who have themselves contributed much to the protection of the Evansville story, William Bartelt and Thomas Lonnberg. Of great significance was the remarkable career of Darrel Bigham, whose meticulous work on the Black community of Evansville was it itself worthy of great acclaim, but who also wrote numerous other books and articles on a wide range of Evansville history topics, as well as playing just about every other role that a professional historian can. Bigham's fine work as Vanderburgh County historian has been carried on by Stan Schmitt. And all these historians have only been able to do their jobs because of the high quality of the archives that exist in the city, tended by generations of librarians and archivists at the Willard Library, the Evansville Vanderburgh Public Library (EVPL), the University of Southern Indiana, the University of Evansville, the Evansville Museum of Arts, History and Science (EMAHS) and the Vanderburgh County Clerk's Archive.

In addition, Evansville's history has been preserved by a truly wonderful group of museums and their staffs, and by two remarkable historical societies. The history collection of the Evansville Museum does an excellent job of telling the story and educating successive generations. The same is true of the Reitz Home Museum, the Evansville African American Museum and the Angel Mounds State Historic Site; all of these places exist only because of the contributions of time, knowledge and money from numerous people over the years. In the recent past, the World War II legacy has been well served by two new museums that will be discussed shortly. There are many communities that lack historical societies, but Evansville has two, both of which are active in offering regular year-round programming in local history. The Vanderburgh County Historical Society (VCHS), founded in the 1880s, and the Southwestern Indiana Historical Society, founded in 1920, also provide funding for worthy local historical causes, and the VCHS has recently made possible literal historic preservation by funding the digitization of several vulnerable movies that are of great significance.

Digitization and video are both essential parts of preventing the loss of any community's history, and Evansville has used both splendidly in recent years. With grant funding from the EVPL Foundation, there is fully searchable full-page access to Evansville newspapers dating to 1871, a phenomenal resource in the battle to preserve the city's past. USI, EMAHS, the Willard Library and the EVPL all also have outstanding collections of digitized photographs and documents dating to the nineteenth century. These include the remarkable collection of photographs from the World War II Evansville shipyard, part of the collection of EMAHS and available on the EVPL website. Through the EVPL, the exhaustive Browning Genealogy Database, the product of the indefatigable Charles Browning, is free and available to the public, averaging over three million visits per year. Another first-class digital resource is HistoricEvansville.com, created and maintained by Joseph Engler, which contains a wealth of information organized in a clear and helpful manner. When it comes to video, Evansville has a unique resource in the Reitz High School Feel the History (FTH) YouTube channel. FTH is a class at Reitz, created by EVSC teachers Jon Carl and Terry Hughes in 2005, where high school students research, write, film, edit and produce documentaries on local history. The students who have gone through the program have made hundreds of films that now reside permanently on YouTube.[481]

Although there are many parts of Evansville's past that could have been lost but have instead been saved, perhaps the clearest example is the story of what Evansville did during World War II, and it is with this example that the book concludes. The city's wartime contribution was staggering, and yet all these efforts, these enormous, literally world-changing efforts, could easily have become lost history. Other than a few fragments and one dilapidated rusting crane, there is nothing physically left of the shipyard. Most of the companies associated with the city's wartime production are long gone from the city or remain in scarcely recognizable forms.[482] Two of Evansville College's war memorials have been lost, the historic marker that stood outside the former Republic Aviation plant has been stolen, the marker at the shipyard is placed in a parking lot that is inaccessible to the public and the Faultless Caster offices were demolished in 2014, ten years after the business ceased operations.[483] As mentioned earlier, two huge critical wartime facilities were destroyed by fire in the winter of 2022. But it is important to note that the loss of this history began almost instantly— Republic Aviation had about one hundred unfinished P-47s in the factory at the end of the war, and most of them—hundreds of truckloads—went to Trockman's junkyard, where they were "sliced into sections with a cutting torch, squashed into 150-pound bales and carted off to the mills for re-melting."[484] Republic gave away a few of the more complete P-47s to local schools, including Evansville College and Mechanic Arts of Evansville, all of which disappeared over the years. In the words of local historian Harold Morgan in 2005,

> *It appears that there are no Evansville-built artifacts of any kind remaining from World War II. It further seems that no keepsakes remain from any of the Tri-State war plants as far as I can report....Our leaders did not have motivation or civic demand to pursue the salvaging of any local war-produced materiel for history.*[485]

The situation had clearly not improved since Pat Wathen's observation, ten years earlier, that despite Evansville's huge contributions, "little evidence remains to remind people what happened here…[and] no single monument of appropriate grandeur exists"[486] The situation was dire.

And yet, in an inspiring example of how things can change, Evansville is now exemplary in ensuring the preservation and communication of the wartime story and in 2022 was designated as Indiana's sole "World War II Heritage City" by the National Parks Service. Harold Morgan and Pat Wathen themselves deserve great credit for not letting the story die over the past thirty years: Morgan published three lavishly illustrated books on the subject, while Wathen's monumental series of articles in the *Courier* marking the fiftieth anniversary of wartime events preserved a vital store of memories. In 1989, the then assistant curator of collections at EMAHS, Thomas Lonnberg, put together an exhibit about the shipyard, based on the museum's collection of 10,467 photographs of the site, donated to them in 1946. Some LST hardware and 70 selected photos went into the exhibit, and in 2013 the Museum opened a permanent gallery dedicated to the wartime contributions of the city.[487] As has been discussed, the entire collection of photographs is now digitized and available online. The last fully operational LST in the world, LST 325, has been permanently docked and open to the public in Evansville since 2005, something that was initially the idea of local historical novelist Mike Whicker. In 2020, thanks to significant local support, it moved to a purpose-built $3.6 million berth with an accompanying museum in the heart of downtown.[488] In 2017, after years of painstaking effort by countless individuals, the Evansville Wartime Museum opened to the public, located close to the Evansville Airport and a stone's throw from the old Republic Aviation plant. In 2020, they were finally able to acquire an Evansville-built P-47 that is one of just four Thunderbolts still flying, and in 2022 they added a functioning Sherman tank, similar to the ones refurbished, rebuilt and tested at the Chrysler plant during the war.[489] Local historians have written books about Evansville in the war, and local experts lecture to the public regularly on the topic. In 1995, WNIN, the local public television station, made a one-hour program called *Evansville War Stories* featuring interviews with veterans and those who were in the city during the war. In 2016, the same broadcaster commissioned a two-hour documentary titled *Evansville at War*; the filmmakers interviewed around forty people to tell the story in their own words.[490] A children's history book donated to all third-grade classrooms in the city as part of Evansville's bicentennial celebrations in 2012 dedicated its entire final chapter to the subject.[491] Far from being lost, the Evansville wartime story is being conserved and is being told louder than ever before.

To communicate why the preservation and propagation of Evansville's history is important, it is appropriate to conclude this book with the words of the great British historian Arthur Marwick:

History is a necessity. Individuals, communities, societies could scarcely exist if all knowledge of the past was wiped out. As memory is to the individual, so history is to the community or society. Without memory, individuals find great difficulty in relating to others, in finding their bearings, and taking intelligent decisions—they lose their sense of identity. A society without history would be in a similar condition....It is only through a sense of history that communities establish their identity, orientate themselves, understand the relationship to the past and to other communities and societies. Without history…we, and our communities, would be utterly adrift on an endless and featureless sea of time.[492]

Without history, we would be *lost*. For the most part, this has not happened in Evansville. Structures have been destroyed, stories have been forgotten, many peoples' lives have ended uncelebrated and unremembered—but thanks to a dedicated band of preservationists, historians, activists and archivists, the wider story of Evansville has not been lost. In this city, the flame of history still burns.

NOTES

Introduction

1. *Reflections Upon a Century*, xi.
2. *Vanderburgh County*, xxviii; Patry, *City of the Four Freedoms*, 12; Bigham, *Evansville Album*, 6; *Evansville Foot by Foot*, 9.
3. "Bank Nearly Ready," *EP*, November 10, 1969.
4. Suarez-Villa, "Regional Inversion in the United States," 429.
5. "Cancellations Take 10,650 Off Pay Rolls," *EC*, August 16, 1945.
6. Patry, *City of the Four Freedoms*, 208–9; Beaven, *We Will Rise*, 17.
7. Petroski, *Road Taken*, 13.
8. "Construction and Destruction," *SCP*, June 20, 1965.

Chapter 1

9. Snow, Gonlin and Siegel, *Archaeology of Native North America*, 207; Madison, *Hoosiers*, 8–9.
10. McCutchan, Bartelt and Lonnberg, *Evansville at the Bend*, 9; Morlock, *Evansville Story*, 5.
11. Black, *Angel Site*, 452–54; Hilgeman, *Pottery and Chronology*, 1.
12. Rogers, "Indian City Evansville's First Subdivision"; Black, *Angel Site*.
13. LaBudde et al., *Angel Mounds*.

14. Runge, "Golf Course Proposed"; Leach, "Commissioners Back Golf Plan"; Allen, *Concept Plan for Development*.

15. Morgan, *Home Town History*, 11–12.

16. Reece, *Who's Who in Evansville*, 6.

17. White and Owen, *Evansville and Its Men*, 9.

18. Patry, *City of the Four Freedoms*, 22, 54–55.

19. Morlock, *Evansville Story*, 44-45.

20. Bigham, *Evansville Album*, 1.

21. Aaron, "Folly of the Big Ditch."

22. Snepp, *Sidelights of Early Evansville History*, 47.

23. "Canal Was a Failure but an Era of Growth Followed," *ECP*, July 3, 1995, 4; Davis, "Boom or Bust."

24. Burns, "$20 Million Ditch."

25. Mellon and Baker, *Evansville Then and Now*, 6; Lannert, *Evansville Courier, Evansville, Indiana*, 5.

26. Goldhor, *First Fifty Years*, 1; Hauton, "Is That a Castle?"; Hall, "Cultural Heritage."

27. "Way Back When," *EP*, July 25, 1965.

28. "100 Years Old: Branch Libraries," *EE*, February 15, 2012.

29. Penland, "About Old North United Methodist."

30. Morlock, *Evansville Story*; Patry, *City of the Four Freedoms*; McCutchan et al, *Evansville*; Barancik, *Jewish Life in Evansville*; *Historic Churches of Evansville*.

31. Gilbert, *History of the City*, 252.

32. Elliott, *History of Evansville and Vanderburgh*, 171.

33. Folz, "School Closings Recall"; "Almost Gone," *EC*, May 30, 1974.

34. "Old Carpenter Biting the Dust," *EP*, December 6, 1961.

35. "High School Enters Advertising Field," *EC*, August 26, 1919.

36. Klinger, *We Face the Future*, 2–8; Olmsted, *From Institute to University*, 88.

37. Elliott, *History of Evansville*, 155; Bartelt, Bartelt and Vanderburgh County Historical Society, *Chronology of the Old Vanderburgh County Courthouse*, 2.

38. "It Is Done. The Work of the Laborer Is Completed at Last," *EC*, November 27, 1890.

39. Morgan, "Evansville."

40. "A Magnificent Work: Completion of the New Jail and Sheriff's Residence," *EJ*, December 24, 1890.

41. Stern and Marchand, nomination form, 8/2.

42. "Old Post Office among Wonders of Evansville," *EP*, July 6, 1984.

43. McCutchan, *From Then Til Now*, 139.

44. Miller, "Evansville Steamboats," 364.

45. Madison, *Indiana Way*, 198.
46. *Roll Call*, 10; *Official Program and Souvenir*, 12.
47. Gilbert, *History of the City*, 278–79; Stern and Marchand, "Oak Hill Cemetery History."
48. Higgins, "Evansville Confederate Monument"; "Oak Hill Cemetery and Arboretum," National Park Service, last modified June 30, 2021, https://www.nps.gov/places/oak-hill-cemetery-and-arboretum.htm.
49. Stern and Marchand, nomination form, 7/3.
50. Bigham, *Evansville*, 7.
51. Patry, *City of the Four Freedoms*, 99–100; Morlock, *Evansville Story*, 110–11.
52. Bosse, *When Everybody Boosts Everybody Wins*, 17; McCutchan, Bartelt and Lonnberg, *Evansville at the Bend*, 40–41.
53. *Karges by Hand*, insert; "Karges Furniture Selling Inventory," *ECP*, August 5, 2014.
54. *Big Beer Doc*.
55. *Book of Evansville*, 4.
56. *Evansville Foot by Foot*.
57. McCutchan, Bartelt and Lonnberg, *Evansville at the Bend*, 49.
58. Casey, "Housing in Evansville," 36–37.
59. Quoted in Barrows, "'Homes of Indiana'," 310.
60. Bacon, *Beauty for Ashes*, 39.
61. Bacon, "Housing Problem," 215.
62. Bigham, "Work, Residence, and the Emergence," 289–90, 308–9.
63. Barrows, "New Deal Public Housing," 55; Sprinkles, *History of Evansville Blacks*, 3–4.
64. Bigham, *We Ask Only a Fair Trial*, 111; "Protest Against Building Is Filed," *EJ*, May 23, 1904.
65. Bigham, "Black Family in Evansville," 169.
66. "To Make Baptisttown a Model Colored Quarter: An Imaginary Sketch of Future Baptistown," *EC*, February 7, 1909, 9. The area is spelled two different ways in the same headline.
67. Madison, *Ku Klux Klan*, 10; Madison, *Hoosiers*, 244.
68. J.C. Kerlin, interview by Darrel Bigham, Oral History Collection, USI Library, March 1974.
69. Wilkinson, "Memories of the Ku Klux Klan," 345–47.
70. Caldemeyer, "Conditional Conservatism," 20; "Enforcement of Law Is Stressed in Klan Meeting," *EJ*, July 18, 1924, 5; "Klan Speakers Outline Policy at Coliseum," *EC*, July 18, 1924, 1.
71. Wilson, "Long, Hot Summer."

72. "Coliseum Is Thronged as Huffington Makes Address," *EJ*, November 3, 1925.
73. Caldemeyer, "Conditional Conservatism," 21; White, *Fragile Alliances*, 66; Madison, *Hoosiers*, 250.
74. Epting, *Roadside Baseball*.
75. Engler, *Evansville*.
76. "Skyscraper Has Fine Appearance," *EC*, January 9, 1916.
77. "A Monument to the Spirit of Enterprise," *EC*, September 26, 1930.
78. Rafford, "10 Most Endangered Properties."
79. Engler, *Evansville*; Morlock, *Evansville Story*, 160–61; Patry, *City of the Four Freedoms*, 129–32.
80. Blackburn and Meyer, *Evansville, Indiana*, 23.
81. "8,082 Go through Turnstiles at the Opening of Bosse Field," *EC*, June 18, 1915.
82. Quoted in Bosse, *When Everybody Boosts*, cover copy.
83. Caldemeyer, "Conditional Conservatism," 6.
84. Bosse, *When Everybody Boosts*, 119, 122.
85. Ibid., 7–8.
86. Bénézet, *1850—One Hundred Years—1950*, 59.
87. Bigham, *Reflections on a Heritage*, 21.
88. White, *Fragile Alliances*, 25.
89. Inglehart, *Account of Vanderburgh County*, 225–26.
90. Gowen, "In Service of Mercy."
91. *In Memoriam*.
92. "Dead 'Boy in Blue' Honored," *EJ*, March 19, 1916; Johnson, *One Hundred Years of Evansville*, 65.
93. Blatt, *Sons of Men*, 75–76.
94. "To Open Gresham Memorial Sunday," *EC*, August 13, 1918; "Honoring James Gresham—Gen. Patton's Grandson, French Dignitary Honor Evansville Man Killed in WWI," *ECP*, November 4, 2017.
95. Keller, *Graham Legacy*, 53–55.
96. Klingler, *How a City Founded*, 62.
97. McCutchan, Bartelt and Lonnberg, *Evansville at the Bend*, 56.
98. "Production of Plymouth Automobiles to Start Soon. Evansville Plant to Turn Out 300 Motor Cars Daily," *Evansville Courier and Journal*, September 1, 1935.
99. "Evansville's 'Dream' Realized," *EJ*, May 17, 1931.
100. "$500,000 Johnson Terminal Will Be Dedicated Today," *EC*, February 27, 1931.

101. "30,000 View Millionth Plymouth in Making," *EC*, March 25, 1953; Coker, "Chrysler Workers Built More"; Klingler, "Chrysler Story in Evansville."

102. *Evansville at War.*

103. Morlock, *Evansville Story*, 191–92; "Two Banks Are Closed by Directors," *EP*, January 12, 1932.

104. "Builders Made Record Feat of Construction," *EC*, September 26, 1930; "Central Union Bank Is Closed for Liquidation," *EC*, January 12, 1932.

105. Tsai, *Development of the Evansville Regional*, 10.

106. Matthews, "Depression Teaches Perspective."

107. Ibid.

108. "Shantytowns Loom as Menace to City's Health, But Officials Puzzle How to Get Rid of Them," *EP*, April 4, 1937.

109. Matthews, "Depression Teaches Perspective."

110. "'Face Lifting' Scheduled for Much of Mesker Park Area in an Extensive Improvement Program Already Under Way by Civilian Conservation Corps," *ECJ*, December 29, 1935; Alexander, *New Jim Crow*, 55.

111. Poletika, "Works Progress Administration Photographs."

112. Baumann, "Legacy of Lily," 37–38, 43.

113. "Official Date Is Compiled in WPA Book. 'Inventory of County Archives' to Be Distributed Soon," *EP*, June 28, 1939; Heiman, "Time Proves New Deal"; Gowen, interview.

114. "The Recreation Department's WPA Band," *EP*, January 26, 1936.

115. Heiman, "Time Proves New Deal," 1; Morlock, *Evansville Story*, 193-5.

116. MacLeod, *Cartoons of Evansville's Karl Kae Knecht*, 71–73; Welky, *Thousand-Year Flood*, xi; Casto, *Great Ohio River Flood*, 7.

117. Davis, "When Disaster Strikes."

118. "The Great Flood of 1937," *Sigeco News* 4, no. 9 (March 1937): 3.

119. "Paul H. Schmidt," *ECP*, November 8, 1999.

120. American National Red Cross, *Evansville's Great Flood*, i, iii, vii.

Chapter 2

121. "Charges Efforts to Get Defense Plants Ignored," *EC*, July 4, 1941.

122. "Move Started to Bring Defense Industries Here," *EC*, July 2, 1941.

123. MacLeod, *Evansville in World War II*, 27.

124. "Navy Will Build Big Shipyard Here," *EC*, February 14, 1942; "Prompt Start on Plane Plant," *EP*, March 23, 1942.

125. Morgan, *Home Front Warriors*, 171–200; Gourley, *Shipyard Work Force*, 163–64.

126. MacLeod, *Evansville in World War II*, 57–59; Stout, *Bullets by the Billion*, foreword; George M. Blackburn, "Hoosier Arsenal," 208.

127. Hyde, *Riding the Roller Coaster*, 145.

128. *The Invader* 3, no. 7 (May 1945); Bigham, *Evansville: World War II*, 53.

129. Morgan, *Home Front Heroes*, 146.

130. Morgan, *Home Front Soldiers*, 207.

131. "County World War II Dead," *EC*, November 10, 1945.

132. White, *Fragile Alliances*, 111, 132; White, "Popular Anticommunism and the UE," 141.

133. MacLeod, *Evansville in World War II*, 63–75; Kersten, *Race, Jobs, and the War*, 68–69.

134. Kennedy, *American People in World War II*, 243.

135. *LST 325*, 119–23.

136. "Evansville Greets Victory with Wild, Noisy Celebration," *EP*, August 15, 1945.

137. Wathen, "August 14, 1945."

138. "Chrysler to Hire 1000 More on Firebomb Job. Produce First Jellied Fire," *EC*, July 18, 1945.

139. Morgan, *Home Front Soldiers*, 204–5.

140. "War Cuts Not to Seriously Affect City," *EP*, August 13, 1945.

141. "5 Plants Hit by Cancellations," *EP*, August 15, 1945.

142. *Evansville at War.*

143. "Cancellations Take 10,650 Off Pay Rolls," *EC*, August 16, 1945; "Chrysler Burns Phosphorus Intended for Use in 1,000,000 Fire Bombs," *EC*, October 18, 1945.

144. "Local Shipyard Declared Surplus," *EC*, September 25, 1945.

145. Tsai, *Development of the Evansville Regional Economy*, 12.

146. *Evansville at War.*

147. Wersich, "LST Production Lines."

148. Klingler, "Wartime Plant Growth."

149. "Refrigerator Making Here Begins Soon," *EC*, August 18, 1945.

150. "Sees New Era Built on Skill Learned in War," *EP*, May 27, 1942.

151. McCabe, *Committee for Economic Development*, 4; Whitham, "Committee for Economic Development," 845–46; "Film Preview for Postwar Planners," *EP*, March 8, 1944.

152. "Mayor Planning Peace Projects," *EP*, March 15, 1943.

153. "Evansville Men Organize to Plan for After War," *EP*, April 27, 1943.

154. "Postwar Plan Need Stressed," *EP*, December 2, 1943.

155. "Nut Club to Aid Post-War Survey," *EC*, February 16, 1944; "Culley Will Attend Postwar Conference," *EP*, April 13, 1944.

156. "Union Leader Says Everyone Has Stake in Conversion," *EP*, July 19, 1944; White, *Fragile Alliances*, 128–29.

157. "Culley Offers Local Postwar Program in Full," *EC*, January 17, 1945.

158. Corrigan, "Prepared for War," *EP*, January 23, 1995; "Culley Offers Local Postwar Program in Full."

159. "Master Plan on Postwar Work to Cost $13,000," *EP*, July 20, 1945.

160. Klingler, *How a City Founded*, 91; Davis, "Rooted in the Fabric."

161. Nickles, "'Preserving Women'," 717; "Millionth Electrolux Brings Jubilation at Servel Plant," *EC*, May 21, 1937; "Plant Merger Is Completed," *EP*, May 14, 1945.

162. "Harvester Firm Buys Republic Plant," *EC*, January 5, 1946; "Local Group Has Worked On Deal for Several Weeks," *EC*, January 5, 1946.

163. Klingler, *How a City Founded*, 64; "Evansville Chrysler Plant," *ECP*, October 13, 2015.

164. "30,000 View Millionth Plymouth in Making," *EC*, March 25, 1953; Coker, "Chrysler Workers Built More"; Klingler, "Chrysler Story in Evansville."

165. Mills and Mills, *Unexpected Journey*, xii, xiv.

166. "War Orders Aiding Job Problem Here," *SCP*, October 28, 1951; Klingler, "Chrysler Story in Evansville"; "Local Aircraft Parts Plants Doubt If They'll Suffer Cuts," *EP*, September 4, 1953; "$21,000,000 Contract for Rifles Given IH," *EC*, July 2, 1953.

167. "1000 Building Wings Here," *EP*, December 18, 1951; "War Work to Increase Jobs Here in '52," *SCP*, December 30, 1951.

168. Tsai, *Development of the Evansville Regional Economy*, 12.

169. Coures, "Sleepwalking City Risks Stubbing."

170. Jackson, *Crabgrass Frontier*, 190–91.

171. Suarez-Villa, "Regional Inversion in the United States," 429.

172. Glaeser and Tobio, "Rise of the Sunbelt," 616.

173. Klingler, "Chrysler Story in Evansville," 15

174. "Last Auto Off the Line Tomorrow," *EP*, August 3, 1959.

175. "Seeger, Whirlpool, RCA Division Directors Approve Merger Plans," *SCP*, July 17, 1955; "Expansion at Seeger to Cost Millions," *EC*, July 18, 1955.

176. "Whirlpool-Seeger Buys Harvester's Plant Here," *EP*, September 27, 1955.

177. Rees, *Refrigeration Nation*, 148–49; Patry, *City of the Four Freedoms*, 206; Nickles, " 'Preserving Women'."

178. "Back-to-Work Move Under Way Here," *SCP*, September 23, 1956.

179. "Servel Completes Sale of Air Conditioning Division," *EC*, September 21, 1957.

180. Townsend, "Whirlpool Gets Servel Appliances."

181. "Disunity, Pessimism Hurt Evansville, Reports Fantus," *EP*, September 9, 1958.

182. Kinoy, "Making of a People's Lawyer," 324.

183. "2 Aides Hurt in Fight at Wallace Meeting," *New York Times*, April 7, 1948; Culver and Hyde, *American Dreamer*, 466–67.

184. Laprade, "Academic Freedom and Tenure," 111; Mills, "'Real Violence at Evansville'"; "IU Instructors Ask Parker Case Action," *Crescent*, May 14, 1948.

185. Foster, "Call Witnesses for UE Red Probe"; White, *Fragile Alliances*, 144.

186. Anderson and Lannert, "State Officers in Full Control"; White, *Fragile Alliances*, 145–49.

187. United States Congress House Committee on Education and Labor, *Investigation of Communist Influence in the Bucyrus-Erie Strike: Hearings Before a Special Subcommittee of the Committee on Education and Labor, House of Representatives, 80th Congress, 2nd Session, Pursuant to H. Res. 111* (1948), 62.

188. Lannert and Foster, "Witnesses Face Contempt Citations"; Klingler, "Secret UE Hearing."

189. Foster and Lannert, "Further UE-CIO Red Probe"; Klingler, "Former Communist Names UE Members."

190. White, *Fragile Alliances*, 150–52; Klingler, "Briggs Unit Refuses to Work."

191. "Evidence of Responsibility," *EC*, July 21, 1955.

192. *Evansville, Indiana.*

193. Klingler, "Hard Facts, Not Sentiment."

194. Klingler, *How a City Founded*, 109.

195. Ed Klinger [Klingler], interviewed by Darrel Bigham, Oral History Collection, USI Library, July 10, 1974.

196. Tsai, *Development of the Evansville Regional Economy*, 11.

197. "Unemployment Rate in Evansville, IN-KY (MSA)," Federal Reserve Economic Data | FRED | St. Louis Fed, last modified April 27, 2022, https://fred.stlouisfed.org/series/EVNURN.

198. McCutchan, Bartelt and Lonnberg, *Evansville at the Bend*, 93.

199. Williams, *Your Career Opportunities.*

200. Fantus Factory Locating Service, *Evansville, Indiana's Potential*, 3–4.

201. "First Alcoa Work Starts," *EC*, July 3, 1956; "First Molten Metal Drawn at Alcoa," *EC*, June 11, 1960.

202. Longest, "'Monster Molders' Thrive"; "Thuerbach Associates launches 'Plastics Valley'," *EC*, January 23, 1987.

203. "Plastics 2nd Biggest Area Employer," *SCP*, July 12, 1973; Tsai, *Development of the Evansville Regional Economy*, 14, 20.

204. Clark, "Mayor Paid Roaring Tribute."

Chapter 3

205. Tucker, "70 Years of Master Plans."

206. Lane, *Houses for a New World*.

207. "Maplewood," *EP*, August 22, 1949.

208. "Prefabricated Homes to Be Built Here," *EC*, June 15, 1946, 5; Derk, "Guthrie Continues Tradition"; Aylsworth, "Guthrie May Was Man."

209. "Guthrie May," *SCP*, July 29, 1984.

210. Corrigan, "Subdivision Builder Bradford Employed."

211. Brown, "Urban Sprawl Has Not Ruined."

212. Grant, "East Side Building Is Story of Progress."

213. "Expansion of Subdivision Planned by Guthrie May," *EC*, August 24, 1954.

214. Martin, "Business Leaders Honored."

215. Diaz, "Homes Mushroom near Newburgh."

216. Carnes, *Columbia History*, 345–46.

217. Aylsworth, "Guthrie May Was Man."

218. Rome, *Bulldozer in the Countryside*, 16; Ventry, "Accidental Deduction," 249–50.

219. Kunstler, *Geography of Nowhere*, 102; Jackson, *Crabgrass Frontier*, 190–218; Lane, *Houses for a New World*, 4–6; Hayden, *Building Suburbia*, 132.

220. Davidson and Sweeney, *On the Move*, 229; Goldfield, *Gifted Generation*, 40.

221. Lang and Sohmer, "Legacy of the Housing Act," 291.

222. "Socialized [Public] Housing Is Not the Answer to Evansville's Housing Problem!" *EC*, April 14, 1952; Hunt, "How Did Public Housing Survive," 193.

223. Wright, "Mild 'Little' Meeting."

224. "First Housing Funds Asked," *EC*, August 4, 1950; "Housing Unit Starts Preliminary Studies," *EC*, December 16, 1965.

225. "Prepares to Name Housing Board," *EP*, September 8, 1942; Perkins, "Local Public Housing Director"; "Tenants for New High-Rise for Elderly May See Apartments Soon," *EC*, September 1, 1972.

226. "Fulton Square Houses Rise Ahead of Schedule," *EP*, July 15, 1956.

227. "'First' Resident Moves into Schnute Towers," *EC*, September 15, 1972; Heiman, "'Decent Place to Live'."

228. Davidson and Sweeney, *On the Move*, 245; Jones, *Slaughter of Cities*, 187, 189.

229. Massey and Tannen, "Suburbanization and Segregation," 1.594.

230. Jacobs, *Detached America*, 29.

231. Hillier, "Residential Security Maps," 207; "Mapping Inequality. Redlining in New Deal America," Digital Scholarship Lab, accessed July 27, 2022, https://dsl.richmond.edu/panorama/redlining/#loc=5/39.1/-94.58.

232. Rothstein, *Color of Law*, 64.

233. Moxley and Fischer, "Historic HOLC Redlining," 1; Hillier, "Residential Security Maps," 208; Aaronson, Hartley and Mazumder, *Effects of the 1930s*, 5; Rutan, "Legacies of the Residential Security Maps," 5.

234. Federal Housing Administration, *Underwriting Manual*, 323.

235. Katznelson, *When Affirmative Action Was White*, 114, 140.

236. Rothstein, *Color of Law*, 64.

237. Moxley and Fischer, "Historic HOLC Redlining," 2. The Evansville map is marked "Prepared by Division of Research and Statistics, With the cooperation of the Appraisal Department, Home Owners' Loan Corporation, June 12, 1937"; Home Owners' Loan Corporation, *NS Form B Area Description Evansville*.

238. "Mapping Inequality."

239. Barrows, "New Deal Public Housing," 52.

240. Bigham, *We Ask Only a Fair Trial*, 219; Wersich, "Lincoln Gardens' Demise."

241. John M. Caldwell, interview by Darrel Bigham, Oral History Collection, USI, July 11, 1973.

242. Pietila, *Not in My Neighborhood*, 50.

243. "Racist Rule Found in Old Evansville HOA Restrictions," *ECP*, September 27, 2019.

244. "Evansville's FIRST Exclusive Subdivision for Colored," *EP*, June 4, 1955; "Area Plan Commission, Vallamar Subdivision," City of Evansville / Vanderburgh County, Indiana, accessed June 2, 2022, https://maps.evansvillegis.com/Apps/Subdivisions/Scans/J/J-028.pdf; Corrigan, "Subdivision Builder Bradford."

245. *Lincolnshire Covenant*; *College Park Association Covenant*. I am grateful to Eric Renschler for bringing these to my attention.

246. "Negro Housing Unit Proposed," *EP*, August 28, 1943.

247. Gugin and Saint Clair, *Indiana's 200*, 290.

248. "Women Charge Public Housing Segregation. Say Evansville Housing Agents Practice Bias," *Indianapolis Recorder*, June 13, 1953; "Suit Asks Negroes in Sweetser Units," *EP*, June 5, 1953; "U.S. Judge Rules Negroes Can Live in Sweetser Units," *EC*, July 7, 1953.

249. "The Human Relations Commission Opens Doors," *EP*, August 13, 1978; "Sweetser Project Is Renamed to Honor Rev. John Caldwell," *EC*, January 21, 1987.

250. Baldwin, *Conversations with James Baldwin*, 42.

251. Ammon, *Bulldozer*, 5.

252. Worthy, *Rape of Our Neighborhoods*; Jones, *Slaughter of Cities*; Jacobs, *Death and Life*, 6; O'Connor, *Building a New Boston*, 284.

253. Harrington, *Other America*, 2–3.

254. Allen, "Pigeon Creek Residents"; "38 Pigeon Creek Shacks Condemned," *EC*, March 26, 1957.

255. "Rising Waters in Pigeon Creek Give Fishermen Much Trouble," *EJ*, April 25, 1901.

256. "In Old Shanty Town…Fire Cleans Up Pigeon Creek," *EP*, January 7, 1955.

257. "Ordinance No 2042," *EC*, May 7, 1953; Perkins, "Legal Action Authorized"; "Notice of Public Hearing on the Project 'B' Urban Renewal Area," *EP*, June 3, 1975.

258. *25 Years of Community Redevelopment*, 1–8, 42.

259. For "Gear Town," see *Evansville at War*; for the other two names, see Klingler, "End of an Era."

260. "Court Notes," *EJ*, October 5, 1874; "City Notes," *EC*, April 25, 1876.

261. "Mayor's Plan Meets Protest," *EJ*, December 2, 1906.

262. "To Segregate Vice of City," *EJ*, July 15, 1906; "Red Light 'Off Again' After Raid by Police," *EC*, October 27, 1953.

263. Jeffries, "Slum Landlords Criticized."

264. Minnis, "Prostitution in Evansville."

265. *25 Years of Community Redevelopment*, 42–43.

266. Spachner, "Residents of Villa Sites"; Garber, "Parkside."

267. "Couple Get Their Dream—A New Home," *EP*, June 22, 1972.

268. Garber, "Parkside."

269. "Inspection, Repair, Razing of Housing Takes Time," *SCP*, July 8, 1962; *25 Years of Community Redevelopment*, 42.

270. Jackson, "Funeral of Villa Sites."

271. Daugherty, "Letter to the Editor."

272. Ibid.

273. Loesch, "'They Just Keep Pushing'."

274. Klingler and Blackburn, "Drive Afoot to Get."

275. "West Side Expressway Route Selected," *SCP*, February 17, 1952.

276. Ibid.

277. "Bridge Called Major Step Toward Boom in Tri-State," *SCP*, July 8, 1956; "Expressway Overpasses Tekoppel Avenue," *EP*, August 19, 1956.

278. Pratt, "Gala Ribbon-Cutting."

279. Jackson, "Hearing Slated on Expressway."

280. Perkins, "Expressway Routing Okayed."

281. Marynell, "For Most, Relocation"; James Derk, "Evansville Will Rejoice"; Bickel, "$160 Million Later."

282. "Relocated Highway 41 to Be Open in Five Months," *SCP*, August 13, 1972.

283. "Boulevard Receives City's 'Green Light'," *EC*, July 9, 1964; "Dedication of Span, Bypass Climaxes States' Program," *EC*, December 17, 1965.

284. "Diamond to be Extended Even if I-64 Isn't," *EP*, June 5, 1975.

285. Wilson, "Tale of Two Highways"; Townsend, "Interstate 64 Battle Continues."

286. "Interstate 64 Southern Route Decided by US Roads Bureau," *EP*, June 21, 1960.

287. Mohl, "Stop the Road," 674–76; Mohl, "Interstates and the Cities," 193–94.

288. Quoted in DiMento and Ellis, *Changing Lanes*, 2.

289. "State Board of Accounts Denies Ruling Against Damages for Overpass," *EP*, March 24, 1955; Flynn, "Delaware Street Overpass"; "City Attorney Says Damages Will Be Paid," *EP*, May 18, 1956.

290. "Protests Closing Third Avenue at Expressway Intersection," *EP*, January 7, 1955; "Expressway Plans Bring Two Protests," *EP*, January 13, 1955; "State to Rule on Expressway Crossing," *EP*, January 21, 1955.

291. Klingler, "Homeowners Claim Loss."

292. Klingler, "State Turns Down Owners."

293. "10,500 Jam City Stadium Dedication," *SCP*, December 2, 1956; "Crowd of 5000 at Opening of Evansville's New Museum," *EC*, October 19, 1959.

294. "$2-Million Bond Plan Is Voted; Sportscenter Would Get Half," *EP*, November 3, 1953; "It's Started," *EP*, March 18, 1955.

295. Robertson, "Overflow Crowd Sees Globetrotters"; "10,500 Jam City Stadium Dedication," *SCP*, December 2, 1956.

296. "Big Gift to Make Possible New Museum Here Is Sought," *EP*, June 16, 1937; "Museum Proposal Grows into Civic Center Idea," *EC*, June 20, 1937.

297. "Anderson Studying Museum Lease," *EP*, July 15, 1957.

298. "Board Okays Sunset Park Museum Site," *EP*, July 26, 1957.

299. "First Dirt Turned for New Museum," *EP*, December 21, 1957; "Crowd of 5000 at Opening of Evansville's New Museum," *EC*, October 19, 1959.

300. "Square Soon to Welcome New Library," *EP*, June 30, 1965; "City's Newest Branch Library Is Dedicated," *EP*, September 9, 1965; "New, Modern Library Will Make Nine in Evansville Public Library System," *SCP*, August 11, 1968; Dezember, "Oaklyn Library Opens"; Howard, *Third Quarter 1962–1987*, 7–10.

301. "Progress in Schools," *SCP*, August 19, 1956.

302. Folz, "Harrison Getting Finishing Touches"; Folz, "New 'Central High'"; Hutchinson, "New School Buildings"; "Progress in Schools," *SCP*, August 19, 1956; *Know Your Schools*, 7–8.

303. Kowalski, *Planning and Managing School Facilities*, 21; Goodnough, "To Build a School."

304. Klinger, *We Face the Future Unafraid*, 84–94.

305. "Kickstarting a Dream," *USI Magazine* 48, no. 2 (2015): 4; "The First Decade: A Step in Time," *8600 University Boulevard* 3, no. 1 (October 1974), 3–4; "Sound Community Investment," *8600 University Boulevard* 4, no. 2 (December 1975), 3; Alley, "First Decade," 4.

306. Coures, "Circle That Wasn't"; Klingler, "Auditorium Now First on List"; Weber, "Yesterday's Freeway Network," 56.

307. Dunning, "New Civic Complex Plan."

308. Klingler, "Many Civic 'Ifs'."

309. Schmitt, "Civic Duty"; Folz, "Civic Center Rates 'Oh's'"; "30,000 Visit Civic Center Open House," *EC*, May 26, 1969.

310. "Groundbreaking Significant for the Future," *EC*, June 21, 1966, 6; Sievers, "Civic Center Construction"; Perkins, "Governor, Sen. Hartke Guests"; Alley, "Center '69 Hallmark."

311. Schrader, "Building Wreckers Show New Concept"; "$25 Million Civic Center Complex Enters First Phase of Construction," *EP*, December 29, 1965.

312. "Fast Face-Lifting Pace Continues," *SCP*, August 14, 1966.

313. Ryder, "Standing Room Only"; "Workman, Spare Those Columns," *EP*, June 17, 1966.

314. Hutchinson, "Tower Razing Ordered"; "Today's the Day," *EP*, September 22, 1973.

315. Ellis, "Cathedral Tolls Own Knell."

316. "Bitterness Envelops Parishoners," *SCP*, January 17, 1965.

317. Ibid.

318. Anderson, *Federal Bulldozer*, 3.

319. Ammon, quoted in Small, "Wastelands of Urban Renewal"; Sievers, "Civic Center Construction"; "Construction and Destruction," *SCP*, June 20, 1965.

320. Byles, *Rubble*, 139.

321. "A Valuable Purchase," *EJ*, January 28, 1890.

322. "Replacement of Buildings Slated for 1970, Downtown," *EC*, January 6, 1970.

323. Schwartz, "Urban Freeways," 238.

324. Ammon, *Bulldozer*, 3.

325. Meredith, "Razing Project to Start."

326. Heiman, "Urban Renewal Issue."

327. "City Clean-up Champion," *Life*, February 17, 1958; Sievers, "Civic Center Construction"; Alley, "End of Era."

328. Ammon, *Bulldozer*, 67.

329. Heiman, "Oakdale Area Forgotten."

330. Alley, "Mayor's Plans."

331. Berry, "McDonald Era Ending."

332. Morgan, "Evansville."

Chapter 4

333. Bailey, *Sex in the Heartland*, 3.

334. "Probe Teen Dope Here, Parents Urge," *EC*, April 20, 1956; "'Pusher' Cites Wide Variety of Illegal Drugs Here," *EC*, August 12, 1973.

335. Baum, "New Jimi Hendrix"; Kennedy, "Alice Struts."

336. Davis, "Memories of Bull Island"; Seits, "Bull Island."

337. "Lively Panel Discussions Held on Obscenity, Abortion Topics," *EC*, January 31, 1972.

338. Barber, "Obscenity Case Filed."

339. Hall, "Pioneers of the Future."

340. Steigerwald, *Sixties and the End*, 95.

341. Hirschman, Preston and Loi, "Vietnamese Casualties," 809.

342. Kirk, "Widow Keeps GI's Image."

343. Melchior, *Legacy of War*, 70–71; Mills and Mills, *Summer Wind*, 232–35.

344. Stanton, "Veterans Day."

345. Gary May, interviewed by Donte Shelton, Oral History Collection, USI, November 5, 2009.

346. Rob Spear, interview with author, Evansville, February 2023.

347. "Antiwar 'Ball' Set for Tonight," *EC*, May 16, 1970; "Peaceniks Say 'Won't Go' by Petition," *Crescent*, March 3, 1970; "Candlelight March Lures 50," *Crescent*, November 18, 1969; Schlepper, "Peace Rally Draws 300."

348. "Quit Vietnam, Urges College Instructor Fiddick," *EP*, January 15, 1965; Flynn, "Teacher at EC."

349. Berger, "Unsigned Editorial"; Bradley, *Upending the Ivory Tower*, 17, 308.

350. "4 Students Slain in Campus Riot," *EC*, May 5, 1970; "Authorities at Kent State Asking 'Why?'," *EP*, May 5, 1970; Ward, *1960s*, 205–6.

351. "Campus Calm Amidst National Violence," *Crescent*, May 12, 1970; "Flag at UE Removed After Scuffle," *EC*, May 9, 1970; Schlepper, "Peace Rally"; "Dismissal Ridiculous," *Crescent*, May 12, 1970; Cowie, "'Hard Hat Riot'."

352. "Candlelight March Lures 50," *Crescent*, November 18, 1969.

353. Levy, *America in the Sixties*, 151; Farber, *Sixties*, 308–9.

354. Wathen, "Twenty Arrested at Rockfest"; "Excise Police Arrest 38 at Bierstube," *EC*, July 2, 1973.

355. Greene, *America in the Sixties*, 137–38.

356. "Sunday Sermon Topics in Evansville Churches," *Evansville Press*, January 1, 1955. The top five denominations in 1955 were as follows: 22 Baptist, 14 Evangelical/Reformed, 13 Lutheran, 12 Methodist, and 9 Presbyterian. "Whatever the Path You Tread, Let That Path Lead to God," *EP*, October 4, 1975, 6. The top four in 1975 were: 14 Southern Baptist, 11 Missouri Synod Lutheran, 11 United Methodist and 9 United Church of Christ.

357. Jackson, "Catholic Diocese Marks Silver Anniversary"; Barancik, Jewish Life in Evansville; McManus, "Moslem Life Workshop."

358. "David Remnick Interview," *NBC Nightly News*, NBC, April 5, 2010.

359. Caldwell, interview.

360. "Pranksters Blamed. Cross Found Burning at Lincoln School," *EP*, July 22, 1964.

361. "City's Blacks Go Back to Its Founding," *EP*, February 25, 1980; Hunt and Weight, "Rediscovering 'Baptistown'," 388.

362. Ellis, "Underground Railroad"; "Funkhouser Legion Post Hall Will be Sold," *EP*, November 17, 1953.

363. "A Diabolical Outrage!! A Negro Outrages a White Woman and Attempts to Murder Her. The Villain Is in Jail," *EDJ*, July 31, 1865.

364. "A Horrible Crime Terribly Expiated," *EDJ*, August 1, 1865.

365. Allen, Als, Lewis and Litwack, *Without Sanctuary*, 13; "Shocking Outrage in Evansville, Ind.," *Chicago Tribune*, August 4, 1865; "Lynch Law," *Chicago Tribune*, August 5, 1865.

366. "Proclamation," *EDJ*, August 2, 1865.

367. Wood, *Lynching and Spectacle*, 4; Apel and Smith, *Lynching Photographs*, 18–20; Dray, *At the Hands*, 7.

368. Campney, "'This Negro Elephant,'" 66–67.

369. "Evansville in the Hands of a Desperate Mob," *EJN*, July 6, 1903.

370. "Anti-Negro Riots in the United States," *Manchester Guardian*, July 8, 1903; "Race War Raging in Evansville. Indiana City Is in the Hands of Mobs," *San Francisco Call*, July 6, 1903; "Evansville's Streets Run with Blood," *Louisville Courier-Journal*, July 7, 1903; "Seven Killed in Evansville Riot," *Minneapolis Journal*, July 7, 1903; "Rioters Shot Dead. Soldiers and Mob in Bloody Clash at Evansville, Ind. Result of a Race War," *Gainesville Star*, July 10, 1903; Butler, *Undergrowth of Folly*, 194.

371. MacLeod, *Cartoons of Evansville's Karl Kae Knecht*, 42–43.

372. Fischer, *Them Damned Pictures*, 81.

373. Boskin, *Sambo*, 14.

374. Bigham, *We Ask Only a Fair Trial*, 116; Loewen, *Sundown Towns*; "Protest Sale of Lots to Negroes," *EJ*, April 6, 1924.

375. Gray, "City's Blacks Go Back."

376. Manuel Milligan, quoted in "Living Close to the Land," *SCP*, December 12, 1971.

377. Gilbert, *History of the City*, 177, 179, 182.

378. "Dr. Gilbert Describes the Awful Tragedy," *EJN*, July 7, 1903; "Blacks, Women Seem Divided on Allegations Against Collier," *ECP*, April 19, 1998.

379. "Former Students Started Mattie Miller Campaign," *ECP*, August 25, 2015.

380. Davis, "For Gold & Glory."

381. Folz, "Negro in Evansville."

382. "Apartment Check Finds Bias Isn't by the Owners," *ECP*, March 7, 1993.

383. Uselton and Densley, "Vandals Hurl Firebombs."

384. "9 Teen Negroes Held in Firebomb Attack on School," *EP*, April 16, 1968; Leach, "2 More Boys"; "Nine Held in Arson at School," *EC*, April 17, 1968.

385. Runge, "Young Negroes Heckle Candidate."

386. "Mayor Promises Probe of Problems at Central," *EC*, October 11, 1968.

387. Folz, "Incidents Bring School Meetings."

388. Berry and Clabes, "Curfew Clamped on City." The English radical Tariq Ali has said of 1968, "Every single month saw an explosion somewhere in the world" (Ali and Watkins, *1968*, 13).

389. "3 Injured in Incidents on Governor," *EC*, August 23, 1968; Schleper, "Police Cruiser"; "Vandalism Continues on Lincoln," *EC*, August 24, 1968.

390. Schleper, "8-to-5 Curfew Imposed."

391. Schleper, "Citizenry Obeys"; "Curfew, Showers Cool City," *SCP*, August 25, 1968.

392. Baskett, "Local Residents Ask"; Folz, "Negroes Charge City Overreacted."

393. Croft, "Racial Violence Here."

394. "Police Without Clues in Boy's Shooting Death," *EP*, July 11, 1969; "City Continues Under Curfew; 25 Persons Jailed. Bullet Only Clue in Boy's Shooting," *EP*, July 12, 1969; "Uneasy Calm Here; 47 Arrested," *SCP*, July 13, 1969; "Curfew Suspended; No New Clues Found," *EP*, July 14, 1969.

395. "Police Steps in Solving Taylor Shooting Traced," *EP*, July 18, 1969.

396. "The Week in Review," 4–5.

397. "Fight Causes Racial Tension at Reitz High," *EP*, October 29, 1971.

398. Folz, "Reitz Negroes Present List"; "To Discuss Grievances HRC, School Officials Meet Students," *EC*, November 3, 1971; "Reitz High Picketed by Negroes," *EP*, November 4, 1971; Folz, "Tension at Reitz."

399. Folz, "Reitz Council Leads Drive."

400. Barber, "Concerned Youth Helps"; Federal Bureau of Investigation, *Counterintelligence Program*.

401. Jones, "Boy Shot by Police"; English, "Grand Jury Finds No Reason"; "Police Board Clears Officers in Shooting," *EP*, November 14, 1973; "Wrongful Death Appeal Rejected," *EP*, January 14, 1980.

402. Leach, "Shooting of Couple Denied," *EC*, October 23, 1974.

403. Jones, "Slaying Called Cause"; Wathen, "Rights Official Believes Gunmen"; "Wounded Negro Teen Dies after Shooting," *EP*, May 8, 1974; Leach, "Officials Alerted to Cope"; Davis, "Wallace Acquitted"; Jones, "Negro Policemen."

404. "Legacy of Terror," *EP*, May 9, 1974.

405. Wathen, "Integration Specialist Arrested"; "Rising Racial Tension Closes Harrison," *EP*, September 20, 1974.

406. "Harrison Opens Quietly Under 'Ground Rules'," *EP*, September 23, 1974.

407. "300 Students Leave Bosse after Unrest," *EP*, September 27, 1974; "Incidents Reported at Bosse," *EC*, September 28, 1974.

408. McConnaughay, "Anguished Bosse Principal."

409. Grehl, "Where Are We."

410. Brown, "9 Central Students Arrested."

411. Sprinkles, *History of Evansville*, 21.

412. Klinger, *We Face the Future Unafraid*, 303; "Evansville College Graduates," *EA*, June 3, 1939; Williams, *Eyes on the Prize*, 10–13; *Our Story*.

413. Culver, "Racial Desegregation in Education," 296–67; Eilidh MacLeod, personal interview, Evansville, March 17, 2021.

414. *Martin v. Evansville-Vanderburgh Sch. Corp.*

415. Hutchinson, "Integration."

416. "Culver School Group Seeks Negro Ban," *EP*, September 12, 1949.

417. "Segregation Group May Take Culver Protest to Court," *EP*, September 13, 1949.

418. "Mayor's Group Okays Plan to End Segregation," *EP*, April 5, 1949.

419. "Picketing Again Today Threatened at School," *EC*, September 21, 1954.

420. "Parents Picket at Harwood in Protest to Negro Pupils," *EP*, September 20, 1954.

421. Ogletree, *All Deliberate Speed*, chapter 1.

422. "Local Schools Well on Way to Achieving Racial Balance," *EP*, February 19, 1970; Folz, "School Plan Supported."

423. Hutchinson, "HEW Drops Order."

424. Hutchinson, "Opposition to Integration Plan."

425. Hutchinson, "HEW Approves Integration"; Hutchinson, "Redistricting Plan Passed"; Cohen, "Integration Plan Protesters Picket"; Hutchinson, "School Board Vetoes."

426. Hutchinson, "Pupil Exchange Plan"; Folz, "It's 'Full Speed Ahead'."

427. "Two Views of Court Order," *EP*, August 12, 1972.

428. Formisano, *Boston Against Busing*, 140.

429. Wallace, "Parents Planning"; Hall, "Freedom School Abandoned"; Delmont, *Why Busing Failed*, 34.

430. "Two Views of Court Order."

431. Jelks, "Letter to the Editor"; Klingler, "Local A.M.E. Pastor Upsets Traditions."

432. Alfred Porter, interview by Darrel Bigham, Oral History Collection, USI, June 12, 1974.

433. "Protest Made on Film Drama," *EC*, November 25, 1915, 23; Hoy, "Civil Rights Movement"; Thornbrough, *Indiana Blacks*, 30.

434. Solomon Stevenson, interviewed by Darrel Bigham, Oral History Collection, USI, November 9, 1972; Caldwell, interview.

435. Stevenson, interview.

436 Porter, interview.

437. Anita Wisdom, interviewed by Jane Egnew, Oral History Collection, USI, June 24, 1974.

438. Folz, "Community Is Challenged."

439. "In Course of Teaching, She Draws Top Grades in Human Rights, Too," *EC*, May 19, 1977; Porter, interview; Charles Rochelle, interview by Darrel Bigham, Oral History Collection, USI, October 5, 1972.

440. "Trial Set Tuesday for Rev. King," *EP*, February 28, 1959; "Prosecutor Drops Rev. King Case," *EP*, March 2, 1959.

441. Folz, "Community Is Challenged."

442. Major H. Alston, interviewed by Darrel Bigham, Oral History Collection, USI, July 20, 1973.

443. "Pastors Set to Join Rights Rally," *EC*, August 26, 1963, 11; Knap, "Local Men Thrilled."

444. Greenwell, "'I Never Felt Any Cold Feet,'" 115, 118, 123; Wilson, "Civil Rights Leader Dies."

445. Swanson, "Black Activist Recalls Evansville."

446. Derk, "Prominent Rights Leader"; Prial, "Charles H. King."

447. Wolcott, "Forgotten History."

448. Wiltse, *Contested Waters*, chapter 5.

449. "Desegregated Swimming at Artes Pool Asked by Negro Recreation Leader," *EC*, June 9, 1956.

450. "Artes Pool Registration Bars Negroes," *EP*, June 11, 1956.

451. "Hearing to Be Set on Segregation Suit," *EP*, June 27, 1956.

452. "City Swim Pools Quiet: De-Segregation Order in Effect," *EC*, July 2, 1956.

453. "Artes Pool Opens, Free of Trouble," *EC*, July 3, 1956; "Negroes Drop Swimming Pool Suit," *EC*, July 4, 1956.

454. "Baptistown Is City's Cancer. Only Cure Is to Cut It Out, Declares Lawrence Veiller, New York Housing Expert," *EC*, May 16, 1916; "Open Housing Law Advised Long Ago," *EC*, November 19, 1968.

455. Folz, "'Open Occupancy' Law"; Runge, "Question of City Ordinance."

456. Carey, "Milwaukee Marchers See City."
457. "NAACP Discusses Open Housing," *EC*, January 5, 1968; "Caldwell to Be Asked Housing Procedures," *EP*, January 5, 1968; Densley, "NAACP Hears Human Relations."
458. Densley, "State Housing Law Backed."
459. "Housing Resolution Approved," *EC*, February 28, 1968, 17.
460. "Meeting with Officials Sought by NAACP," *EP*, August 2, 1968.
461. "Text of Negroes' Demands Submitted to City Council," *EP*, August 29, 1968.
462. Pampe, "Open Housing Ordinance."
463. Pampe, "Open Housing Measure."
464. Perkins, "Housing Ordinance Amendments."
465. Runge, "Clergymen Call"; Runge, "Bar Group Will Give Housing."
466. "Housing Ordinance OK Urged," *EC*, October 29, 1968; "Petition Asks Strong Local Open Housing," *EP*, November 6, 1968.
467. "Tough Open Housing Ordinance Made Official by City Council," *EP*, November 19, 1968; Pampe, "Local Open Housing Ordinance"; "12-Year Councilman Out of the Spotlight but Still Busy," *EP*, October 22, 1985.
468. Folz, "Forceful Fighter Passes."
469. Vinen, *1968*; Zelizer, *Fierce Urgency of Now*, 296–97.
470. *Resolution Memorializing the 50th Anniversary*.
471. Wallis, *America's Original Sin*, 43.

Conclusion

472. Brad Collins, "'Recycling Past'."
473. "Historic Savers, Welcome," *EP*, April 22, 1972.
474. Hill, "Preservation Proposal Meets Opposition."
475. Stems, "Wesselman Park Planned"; Morlock, "Wesselman Park and Nature Preserve," 18; Brenneman, "Natural and Cultural History."
476. Bigham, *Evansville*, 6.
477. Armstrong, "Honorees Cite Notable Preservation."
478. "Marchand Honored for Her Local Efforts in Preserving History," *EP*, May 5, 1995.
479. Armstrong, "Restoration Projects."
480. "Historic Preservation Expert Marchand Dies," *EP*, January 3, 1997; McBain, "Looking into the Past."

481. Carl, "FJ Reitz High School."

482. MacLeod, *Evansville in World War II*, 118–20.

483. "'This Place Has a Soul' Faultless Caster Building Demolished After Century," *ECP*, June 6, 2014.

484. "$40,000 P-47s Bring $125 as War Tools Are Junked for Plowshares," *EP*, October 11, 1945.

485. Morgan, "Tri-State's War Effort."

486. Wathen, "Evansville Needs Grand Reminder."

487. McBain, "Shipyard Pictures Could Refocus."

488. Seibert, "LST 325 Welcomed."

489. "Evansville Wartime Museum to open for public," *ECP*, May 24, 2017, 3; Doyle, "Evansville's Own P-47"; "Historic WWII Tank Collected by Evansville Wartime Museum," Eyewitness News (WEHT/WTVW), last modified May 25, 2022, https://www.tristatehomepage.com/news/local-news/historic-wwii-tank-collected-by-evansville-wartime-museum/.

490. Wathen, "WNIN's 'War Stories'"; *Evansville at War*.

491. Karcher, *Where the River Grins*.

492. Marwick, *New Nature of History*, 31–32.

BIBLIOGRAPHY

News Sources

Chicago Tribune
8600 University Boulevard
Evansville Argus
Evansville Courier
Evansville Courier and Journal
Evansville Courier and Press
Evansville Daily Journal
Evansville Examiner
Evansville Journal
Evansville Journal-News
Evansville Press
Eyewitness News
Gainesville Star

Indianapolis Recorder
The Invader
Louisville Courier-Journal
Manchester Guardian
Minneapolis Journal
NBC News
New York Times
San Francisco Call
Sigeco News
Sunday Courier and Press
University of Evansville Crescent
USI Magazine

Archival Records

City of Evansville
US Federal Reserve
USI Oral History Collection
Vanderburgh County

Printed Sources

Aaron, Joe. "The Folly of the Big Ditch." *ECP*, May 17, 2009.

Aaronson, Daniel, Daniel Hartley and Bhashkar Mazumder. *The Effects of the 1930s HOLC "Redlining" Maps*. Chicago: Federal Reserve Bank of Chicago, 2017.

Alexander, Michelle. *The New Jim Crow: Mass Incarceration in the Age of Colorblindness*. 3rd ed. New York: New Press, 2020.

Ali, Tariq, and Susan Watkins. *1968: Marching in the Streets*. New York: Free Press, 1998.

Allen, F.E. *Concept Plan for Development of Angel Mounds Park and State Memorial*. Bennington, VT: Allen Organization, 1964.

Allen, Glenn. "Pigeon Creek Residents Get Official Notice." *EP*, March 25, 1957.

Allen, James, Hilton Als, John Lewis and Leon F. Litwack. *Without Sanctuary: Lynching Photography in America*. Santa Fe, NM: Twin Palms Publishing, 2000.

Alley, Homer. "Center '69 Hallmark." *SCP*, August 17, 1969.

———. "End of Era: Villa Sites Going Down." *SCP*, September 15, 1968.

———. "The First Decade." *8600 University Boulevard* 4, no. 2 (December 1975): 4.

———. "Mayor's Plans 'Go'." *SCP*, August 17, 1969.

American National Red Cross, Evansville Chapter, Archives Commission. *Evansville's Great Flood, 1937: History of the Flood, Evansville Area, January–February 1937*. Evansville, IN: University of Evansville, 1977.

Ammon, Francesca R. *Bulldozer: Demolition and Clearance of the Postwar Landscape*. New Haven, CT: Yale University Press, 2016.

Anderson, Martin. *The Federal Bulldozer: A Critical Analysis of Urban Renewal, 1949–1962*. Cambridge: MIT Press, 1964.

Anderson, Rodney, and Hallie B. Lannert. "State Officers in Full Control at Bucyrus-Erie," *EC*, September 1, 1948.

Apel, Dora, and Shawn M. Smith. *Lynching Photographs*. Oakland: University of California Press, 2007.

Armstrong, Dan. "Honorees Cite Notable Preservation Wins, Losses." *EP*, May 13, 1998.

———. "Restoration Projects Earn Preservation Rewards." *EP*, May 9, 1997.

Aylsworth, Jan. "Guthrie May Was Man of Integrity." *SCP*, July 29, 1984.

Bacon, Albion F. *Beauty for Ashes, with Numerous Illustrations*. New York: Dodd, Mead and Company, 1914.

———. "The Housing Problem." *Indiana Bulletin of Charities and Correction*, June 1909, 212–19.

Bailey, Beth L. *Sex in the Heartland*. Cambridge, MA: Harvard University Press, 2009.

Baldwin, James. *Conversations with James Baldwin*. Jackson: University Press of Mississippi, 1989.

Barancik, Sue. *Jewish Life in Evansville 1857–2007: A Brief History of the Jewish Community in Evansville, Indiana*. Evansville, IN: Temple Adath B'nai Israel, 2007.

Barber, Joe. "Concerned Youth Helps Cool Potentially Violent Night." *EP*, June 22, 1973.

———. "Obscenity Case Filed Against 2." *EP*, April 13, 1972.

Barrows, Robert G. "'The Homes of Indiana': Albion Fellows Bacon and Housing Reform Legislation, 1907–1917." *Indiana Magazine of History* 81, no. 4 (December 1985): 309–50.

———. "New Deal Public Housing in the Ohio Valley: The Creation of Lincoln Gardens in Evansville, Indiana." *Ohio Valley History* 14, no. 1 (Spring 2014): 51–72.

Bartelt, William, Kathryn Bartelt and Vanderburgh County Historical Society. *A Chronology of the Old Vanderburgh County Courthouse, Jail, and Sheriff's Residence*. Evansville, IN: Vanderburgh County Historical Society, 1990.

Baskett, Doug. "Local Residents Ask 'Why Did It Happen?'" *EP*, August 26, 1968.

Baum, Susan. "New Jimi Hendrix Slightly Tamer Variety." *EP*, June 11, 1970.

Baumann, Timothy E. "The Legacy of Lily, Black, and the WPA at Angel Mounds near Evansville, Indiana." *The SAA Archeological Record* 11, no. 5 (November 2011): 34–38.

Beaven, Steve. *We Will Rise: A True Story of Tragedy and Resurrection in the American Heartland*. New York: Little A, 2020.

Bénézet, Louis P. *1850—One Hundred Years—1950: A River, a City and a Bank; a Story of the Growth Through Faith, Courage, Integrity and Service*. Evansville, IN: National City Bank, 1950.

Berger, Charles. "Unsigned Editorial." *The Iconoclast* (Evansville, IN), April 23, 1969.

Berry, David. "McDonald Era Ending: Part II." *EC*, December 24, 1971.

Berry, David, and Gene Clabes. "Curfew Clamped on City Second Straight Night." *EC*, August 26, 1968.

Bickel, Cheryl. "$160 Million Later, Lloyd Expressway Opens to Traffic." *EP*, July 19, 1988.

The Big Beer Doc. Directed by Joe Atkinson. 2018. Evansville: WNIN/Court Street Productions, Film.

Bigham, Darrel E. "The Black Family in Evansville and Vanderburgh County, Indiana: A 1900 Postscript." *Indiana Magazine of History* 78, no. 2 (June 1982): 154–69.

———. *Evansville.* Charleston, SC: Arcadia Publishing, 1998.

———. *An Evansville Album: Perspectives on a River City, 1812–1988.* Bloomington: Indiana University Press, 1988.

———. *Evansville: The World War II Years.* Charleston, SC: Arcadia Publishing, 2005.

———. *Reflections on a Heritage: The German Americans in Southwestern Indiana.* Evansville, IN: N.p., 1980.

———. *We Ask Only a Fair Trial: A History of the Black Community of Evansville, Indiana.* Bloomington: Indiana University Press, 1987.

———. "Work, Residence, and the Emergence of the Black Ghetto in Evansville, Indiana, 1865–1900." *Indiana Magazine of History* 76, no. 4 (December 1980): 287–318.

Black, Glenn A. *Angel Site, Vanderburgh County, Indiana: An Introduction.* Indianapolis: Indiana Historical Society, 1944.

Blackburn, George M. "The Hoosier Arsenal." PhD diss., Indiana University, 1957.

Blackburn, Tom, and Henry A. Meyer. *Evansville, Indiana, 1812–1962.* Evansville, IN: Evansville Sesquicentennial Commission, 1962.

Blatt, Heiman. *Sons of Men: Evansville's War Record.* Evansville, IN: Abe P. Madison, 1920.

The Book of Evansville, Illustrated. Evansville, IN: Worthington Engraving Company, 1895.

Boskin, Joseph. *Sambo: The Rise and Demise of an American Jester.* New York: Oxford University Press, 1988.

Bosse, Jeffrey A. *When Everybody Boosts Everybody Wins: The Untold Story of Evansville Mayor Benjamin Bosse.* Evansville, IN: M.T. Publishing, 2014.

Bradley, Stefan M. *Upending the Ivory Tower: Civil Rights, Black Power, and the Ivy League.* New York: New York University Press, 2018.

Brenneman, James. "Natural and Cultural History of Wesselman Park." Lecture, 25th Anniversary of the Opening of Wesselman Park Nature Center, Evansville, 1978.

Brown, Andrea. "Urban Sprawl Has Not Ruined Iroquois Gardens." *EP,* June 20, 1989.

Brown, Janice. "9 Central Students Arrested in Fracas." *EC,* November 7, 1975.

Burns, Mike. "$20 Million Ditch. Wabash-Erie Canal." *SCP*, October 22, 1967.

Butler, Brian. *An Undergrowth of Folly: Public Order, Race Anxiety, and the 1903 Evansville, Indiana Riot*. New York: Garland, 2000.

Byles, Jeff. *Rubble: Unearthing the History of Demolition*. Danvers: Crown, 2007.

Caldemeyer, Dana M. "Conditional Conservatism. Evansville, Indiana's Embrace of the Ku Klux Klan, 1919–1924." *Ohio Valley History* 11, no. 4 (Winter 2011): 3–24.

Campney, Brent M. "'This Negro Elephant Is Getting to Be a Pretty Large Sized Animal': White Hostility against Blacks in Indiana and the Historiography of Racist Violence in the Midwest." *Middle West Review* 1, no. 2 (Spring 2015): 63–91.

Carey, Ann. "Milwaukee Marchers See City as Symbol." *EP*, October 14, 1967.

Carl, Jon. "FJ Reitz High School Feel the History." YouTube. Accessed August 25, 2022. https://www.youtube.com/user/FeeltheHistory.

Carnes, Mark C., ed. *The Columbia History of Post-World War II America*. New York: Columbia University Press, 2007.

Casey, Ray D. "Housing in Evansville." Master's thesis, Indiana University, 1916.

Casto, James E. *The Great Ohio River Flood of 1937*. Charleston, SC: Arcadia Publishing, 2009.

Clark, Jim. "Mayor Paid Roaring Tribute." *EC*, October 11, 1963.

Cohen, Steve. "Integration Plan Protesters Picket Homes." *EP*, June 21, 1972.

Coker, David. "Chrysler Workers Built More Than Cars." *ECP*, October 22, 2011.

College Park Association Covenant. Evansville, IN: Vanderburgh County, n.d.

Collins, Brad. "'Recycling Past.' Evansville Becoming Aware of Its Cultural Heritage." *EP*, May 7, 1977.

Corrigan, Sara A. "Prepared for War but Not Peace?" *EP*, January 23, 1995.

———. "Subdivision Builder Bradford Employed Ideas Ahead of His Time." *EP*, June 20, 1989.

Coures, Kelley. "The Circle That Wasn't." *Evansville Living*, November 13, 2014.

———. "Sleepwalking City Risks Stubbing Its Toe on Reality." *ECP*, September 12, 2007.

Cowie, Jefferson. "The 'Hard Hat Riot' Was a Preview of Today's Political Divisions." *New York Times*, May 11, 2020.

Croft, Joe H., III. "Racial Violence Here Held 'Ominously Near'." *EC*, August 11, 1966.

Culver, Dwight W. "Racial Desegregation in Education in Indiana." *Journal of Negro Education* 23, no. 3 (1954): 296–302.

Culver, John C., and John Hyde. *American Dreamer: A Life of Henry A. Wallace*. New York: W.W. Norton & Company, 2001.

Daugherty, Delores. "Letter to the Editor: Houses in Villa Sites." *EC*, October 20, 1955.

Davidson, Janet F., and Michael S. Sweeney. *On the Move: Transportation and the American Story*. Washington, DC: National Geographic Society, 2003.

Davis, Rich. "Boom or Bust. The Failed Wabash and Erie Canal Helped Put Evansville on the Map." *ECP*, August 13, 1995.

———. "For Gold & Glory—In the 1920s, Blacks Barred from the Indy 500 Became Barnstorming Heroes, Led by a Speed King From Evansville." *ECP*, May 18, 2003.

———. "Memories of Bull Island 1972." *EC*, September 6, 1992.

———. "Rooted in the Fabric of the Community." *ECP*, April 11, 2010.

———. "Wallace Acquitted in Slaying." *EC*, August 23, 1974.

———. "When Disaster Strikes—Life Came to a Halt as 1937 Flood Hit Region." *ECP*, January 7, 2007.

Delmont, Matthew F. *Why Busing Failed: Race, Media, and the National Resistance to School Desegregation*. Oakland: University of California Press, 2016.

Densley, Dick. "NAACP Hears Human Relations Unit Hit." *EC*, February 2, 1968.

———. "State Housing Law Backed." *EC*, February 6, 1968.

Derk, James. "Evansville Will Rejoice Over the Completion of the Russell Lloyd Expressway on Tuesday." *Sunday Courier*, July 17, 1988.

———. "Guthrie Continues Tradition." *Sunday Courier*, October 25, 1987.

———. "Prominent Rights Leader Charles King Dies." *EC*, September 15, 1991.

Dezember, Mary. "Oaklyn Library Opens Thursday." *SCP*, December 29, 1974.

Diaz, Sally K. "Homes Mushroom near Newburgh." *EP*, December 18, 1970.

DiMento, Joseph F., and Cliff Ellis. *Changing Lanes: Visions and Histories of Urban Freeways*. Cambridge: MIT Press, 2013.

Doyle, Michael. "Evansville's Own P-47 Tarheel Hal Returns—Aircraft Gets Huge Welcome as It Lands at New Home." *EC*, October 19, 2020.

Dray, Philip. *At the Hands of Persons Unknown: The Lynching of Black America*. New York: Modern Library, 2007.

Dunning, Albert C. "New Civic Complex Plan Is Considered." *EP*, July 12, 1963.

Elliott, Joseph P. *A History of Evansville and Vanderburgh County, Indiana: A Complete and Concise Account from the Earliest Times to the Present, Embracing Reminiscences of the Pioneers and Biographical Sketches of the Men Who Have Been Leaders in Commercial and Other Enterprises.* Evansville, IN: Keller Printing Company, 1897.

Ellis, James F. "Cathedral Tolls Own Knell," *SCP*, January 17, 1965.

———. "The Underground Railroad." *SCP*, May 8, 1966.

Engler, Joe. "Historic Evansville." Historic Evansville. Accessed May 31, 2022. https://www.historicevansville.com/railroad.php.

Engler, Joseph. *Evansville*. Charleston, SC: Arcadia Publishing, 2012.

English, Terry. "Grand Jury Finds No Reason to Indict Patrolman in Fatal Shooting of Youth." *EP*, November 5, 1973.

Epting, Chris. *Roadside Baseball: The Locations of America's Baseball Landmarks.* Solana Beach, CA: Santa Monica Press, 2009.

Evansville at War. Directed by Joe Atkinson, and James MacLeod. 2016. Evansville: WNIN PBS, DVD.

Evansville Foot by Foot: Walk the Riverside Historic District. Evansville, IN: Evansville Convention and Visitors Bureau, 1999.

Evansville, Indiana: Balance Point, USA. 1954. Committee of 100, Film.

Fantus Factory Locating Service. *Evansville, Indiana's Potential for Industrial Growth: A Community Appraisal.* Chicago: Fantus, 1958.

Farber, David, ed. *The Sixties: From Memory to History.* Chapel Hill: University of North Carolina Press Books, 2012.

Federal Bureau of Investigation. *Counterintelligence Program. Black Nationalist–Hate Groups.* Washington, DC: U.S. Department of Justice, 1971.

Federal Housing Administration. *Underwriting Manual: Underwriting and Valuation Procedure Under Title II of the National Housing Act.* Washington, DC: Federal Housing Administration, 1936.

Fischer, Roger A. *Them Damned Pictures: Explorations in American Political Cartoon Art.* North Haven, CT: Archon Books, 1996.

Flynn, Robert. "Delaware Street Overpass Families Can't Get Damages. Wall Blocks Frontages." *EP*, March 22, 1955.

———. "Teacher at EC Plans to Form Anti-War Unit." *EP*, November 30, 1965.

Folz, Edna. "Civic Center Rates 'Oh's' and 'Ah's'." *EP*, May 24, 1969.

———. "Community Is Challenged to Give Negro Equal Place, End 'Vestiges of Segregation'." *EP*, August 13, 1959.

————. "Forceful Fighter Passes: Leukemia Fatal to Man of Action." *EP*, December 4, 1970.

————. "Harrison Getting Finishing Touches." *EP*, August 25, 1962.

————. "Incidents Bring School Meetings; Game Postponed." *EP*, October 12, 1968.

————. "It's 'Full Speed Ahead' for School Balance Plan." *EP*, August 12, 1972.

————. "Negroes Charge City Overreacted." *EP*, August 24, 1968.

————. "The Negro in Evansville…5½ Years Later." *EP*, August 11, 1969.

————. "New 'Central High' to Cost $7.5 Million." *EP*, January 18, 1968.

————. "'Open Occupancy' Law Is Believed Invalid." *EP*, April 1, 1964.

————. "Reitz Council Leads Drive for a Better Race Relations." *EP*, November 11, 1971.

————. "Reitz Negroes Present List of Complaints." *EP*, November 2, 1971.

————. "School Closings Recall Their Origins." *EP*, June 6, 1972.

————. "School Plan Supported." *EP*, December 18, 1969.

————. "Tension at Reitz—How It Grew." *EP*, November 10, 1971.

Formisano, Ronald P. *Boston Against Busing: Race, Class, and Ethnicity in the 1960s and 1970s*. Chapel Hill: University of North Carolina Press, 2012.

Foster, Fred. "Call Witnesses for UE Red Probe at 10am Friday." *EC*, September 9, 1948.

Foster, Fred, and Hallie Lannert. "Further UE-CIO Red Probe Looms." *SCP*, August 12, 1948.

Garber, Kim. "Parkside: More Than Name Changed." *EP*, April 30, 1974.

Gilbert, Frank M. *History of the City of Evansville and Vanderburg County, Indiana*. Chicago: Pioneer Publishing, 1910.

Glaeser, Edward, and Kristina Tobio. "The Rise of the Sunbelt." *Southern Economic Journal* 74, no. 3 (January 2008): 609–43.

Goldfield, David. *The Gifted Generation: When Government Was Good*. New York: Bloomsbury Publishing, 2017.

Goldhor, Herbert. *The First Fifty Years: The Evansville Public Library and the Vanderburgh County Public Library*. Evansville, IN, 1962.

Goodnough, Abby. "To Build a School." *New York Times*, October 6, 1996.

Gourley, Harold E. *Shipyard Work Force: World's Champion LST Builders on the Beautiful Ohio, 1942–1945, Evansville, IN*. Mount Vernon, IN: Windmill Publications, 1996.

Gowen, Amber. "In Service of Mercy: Evansville World War I Nurses." Evansville Wartime Museum. Accessed July 8, 2022. https://www.evansvillewartimemuseum.org/in-service-of-mercy-2/.

————. Interview with author. Evansville. August 3, 2022.

Grant, William. "East Side Building Is Story of Progress." *SCP*, October 31, 1948.

Gray, Emma Grimes. "City's Blacks Go Back to Its Founding." *EP*, February 25, 1980.

Greene, John R. *America in the Sixties*. Syracuse, NY: Syracuse University Press, 2010.

Greenwell, Ava T. "'I Never Felt Any Cold Feet.' How Age, Gender, and Family Background Shaped the Sit-In Movement in Henderson, Kentucky." *Souls* 15, no. 1–2 (2013): 110–32.

Grehl, Michael. "Where Are We Now?" *EP*, September 28, 1974.

Gugin, Linda C., and James E. Saint Clair. *Indiana's 200: The People Who Shaped the Hoosier State*. Indianapolis: Indiana Historical Society, 2016.

Hall, Bob. "Pioneers of the Future." *SCP*, November 15, 1970.

Hall, Robert N. "Cultural Heritage." *SCP*, October 29, 1972.

Hall, Steve. "Freedom School Abandoned This Year." *SCP*, October 22, 1972.

Harrington, Michael. *The Other America: Poverty in the United States*. New York: Macmillan, 1962.

Hauton, Bob. "Is That a Castle?" *EP*, March 1, 1959.

Hayden, Dolores. *Building Suburbia: Green Fields and Urban Growth, 1820–2000*. New York: Vintage, 2009.

Heiman, Roberta. "'A Decent Place to Live'." *EP*, February 21, 1973.

———. "Oakdale Area Forgotten." *EP*, December 10, 1971.

———. "Time Proves New Deal Was a Good Deal." *Sunday Courier*, January 8, 1989.

———. "The Urban Renewal Issue. Is Bulldozer Only Answer?" *EP*, July 5, 1975, 1.

Higgins, Jessie. "Evansville Confederate Monument Lacking Controversy." *ECP*, August 20, 2017.

Hilgeman, Sherri L. *Pottery and Chronology of the Angel Site, a Middle Mississippian Center in the Lower Ohio Valley*. Tuscaloosa: University of Alabama Press, 2000.

Hill, Scott P. "Preservation Proposal Meets Opposition from Area Residents." *EC*, August 14, 1974.

Hillier, Amy E. "Residential Security Maps and Neighborhood Appraisals: The Home Owners' Loan Corporation and the Case of Philadelphia." *Social Science History* 29, no. 2 (Summer 2005): 207–33.

Hirschman, Charles, Samuel Preston and Vu M. Loi. "Vietnamese Casualties During the American War: A New Estimate." *Population and Development Review* 21, no. 4 (December 1995): 783–812.

Historic Churches of Evansville. n.d. Evansville: WNIN, 2022. Film.

History of Vanderburgh County, Indiana, from Earliest Times to the Present: With Biographical Sketches, Reminiscences, Etc. Madison, WI: Grant and Fuller, 1889.

Home Owners' Loan Corporation. *NS Form B Area Description Evansville–Indiana: Area No. D-6*. Washington, DC: U.S. Government Printing Office, 1937.

Howard, E.A. *The Third Quarter 1962–1987: An Account of the History of the Evansville-Vanderburgh County Public Library*. Evansville, IN: Evansville-Vanderburgh Public Library, 1987.

Hoy, Philip. "Civil Rights Movement in the 1960s Did Not Pass Us By." *EP*, January 27, 1990.

Hunt, D.B. "How Did Public Housing Survive the 1950s?" *Journal of Policy History* 17, no. 2 (2005): 193–216.

Hunt, Tamara L., and Donovan Weight. "Rediscovering 'Baptistown': A Historical Geography Project on Local African American History." *History Teacher* 51, no. 3 (May 2018): 387–408.

Hutchinson, Nancy. "HEW Approves Integration Plan." *EC*, February 3, 1972.

———. "HEW Drops Order for School Busing." *EC*, September 29, 1971.

———. "Integration: 25 Years of Change." *EC*, March 8, 1974.

———. "New School Buildings Set Record." *EC*, August 31, 1971.

———. "Opposition to Integration Plan Forming." *EC*, November 20, 1971.

———. "Pupil Exchange Plan Ordered Reinstated." *EC*, August 12, 1972.

———. "Redistricting Plan Passed By School Board." *EC*, May 11, 1972.

———. "School Board Vetoes Pupil Exchange." *EC*, August 3, 1972.

———. "Tower Razing Ordered." *EC*, September 20, 1973.

Hyde, Charles K. *Riding the Roller Coaster: A History of the Chrysler Corporation*. Detroit, MI: Wayne State University Press, 2003.

Inglehart, John E. *An Account of Vanderburgh County from Its Organization*. Dayton, OH: Dayton Historical Publishing, 1923.

In Memoriam: Albert Craig Funkhouser (Co. F, 144 Inf., 36th Division), Paul Taylor Funkhouser (Co. B, 7th Machine Gun Bn., 3rd Division). Evansville, IN: 1919.

Jackson, Chuck. "Catholic Diocese Marks Silver Anniversary Week." *EC*, November 14, 1969.

———. "Funeral of Villa Sites," *EC*, October 22, 1971.

Jackson, Jari. "Hearing Slated on Expressway." *EC*, February 21, 1964.

Jackson, Kenneth T. *Crabgrass Frontier: The Suburbanization of the United States*. New York: Oxford University Press, 1985.

Jacobs, James A. *Detached America: Building Houses in Postwar Suburbia.* Charlottesville: University of Virginia Press, 2015.

Jacobs, Jane. *The Death and Life of Great American Cities.* New York: Vintage, 1992.

Jeffries, Phil. "Slum Landlords Criticized. Housing Aide Seeks More Speed in Slum Fight." *SCP*, March 17, 1963.

Jelks, Arthur L. "Letter to the Editor: Thanks Police." *EP*, March 30, 1956.

Johnson, Charles E. *One Hundred Years of Evansville, Indiana, 1812–1912 with Miscellanea.* Evansville, IN: N.p., 1948.

Jones, E.M. *The Slaughter of Cities: Urban Renewal as Ethnic Cleansing.* South Bend, IN: Fidelity Press, 2004.

Jones, Mike. "Boy Shot by Police Dies after Surgery." *EP*, October 11, 1973.

———. "Negro Policemen on Case." *EP*, May 9, 1974.

———. "Slaying Called Cause of Shootings." *EP*, May 4, 1974.

Karcher, Angie. *Where the River Grins: The History of Evansville, Indiana.* Evansville, IN: MT Publishing, 2012.

Karges By Hand. Evansville, IN: Karges Furniture Company, n.d.

Katznelson, Ira. *When Affirmative Action Was White: An Untold History of Racial Inequality in Twentieth-Century America.* New York: W.W. Norton & Company, 2006.

Keller, Michael E. *The Graham Legacy: Graham-Paige to 1932.* Paducah, KY: Turner Publishing Company, 1998.

Kennedy, David M. *The American People in World War II: Freedom from Fear, Part Two.* New York: Oxford University Press, 2003.

Kennedy, Ridge. "Alice Struts, Frets, in Brand New Style." *EP*, March 28, 1975.

Kersten, Andrew E. *Race, Jobs, and the War: The FEPC in the Midwest, 1941–46.* Champaign: University of Illinois Press, 2000.

Kinoy, Arthur. "The Making of a People's Lawyer." *Science and Society* 45, no. 3 (Fall 1981).

Kirk, Cynthia. "Widow Keeps GI's Image Alive for Son." *EP*, May 29, 1972.

Klinger, George. *We Face the Future Unafraid: A Narrative History of the University of Evansville.* Evansville, IN: University of Evansville Press, 2003.

Klingler [Klinger], Ed. "Auditorium Now First on List of Civic Circle Building Project." *EP*, March 13, 1963.

———. "Briggs Unit Refuses to Work with Man Identified as Red." *EP*, September 12, 1948.

———. "The Chrysler Story in Evansville—An Asset for 24 Years." *EP*, July 30, 1959.

———. "The End of an Era. Infamous 'District' in Path of Progress." *EP*, August 5, 1957.

———. "Former Communist Names UE Members Here." *EP*, September 11, 1948.

———. "Hard Facts, Not Sentiment, to Govern Chrysler's Verdict." *EP*, October 1, 1957.

———. "Homeowners Claim Loss Caused by Expressway." *EP*, June 7, 1957.

———. *How a City Founded to Make Money Made It: The Economic and Business History of Evansville, Indiana*. Evansville, IN: University of Evansville, 1976.

———. "Local A.M.E. Pastor Upsets Traditions in Constant Battle for Negro Rights." *EP*, July 16, 1957.

———. "Many Civic 'Ifs' Could Have Blocked Today's Civic Center." *EP*, May 23, 1969.

———. "Secret UE Hearing Asked for Workers 'Who Fear Revenge'." *EP*, September 10, 1948.

———. "State Turns Down Owners on Expressway Damage Plea." *EP*, August 28, 1957.

———. "Wartime Plant Growth Points Toward More Peacetime Jobs." *EP*, August 17, 1945.

Klingler, Ed, and Tom Blackburn. "Drive Afoot to Get 41 in Road System," *EP*, April 28, 1960.

Knap, Ted. "Local Men Thrilled by March." *EP*, August 28, 1963.

Know Your Schools. A Booklet of Information About the Evansville-Vanderburgh School Corporation. Evansville, IN: League of Women Voters Education Fund, 1976.

Kowalski, Theodore J. *Planning and Managing School Facilities*. Santa Barbara, CA: Greenwood Publishing Group, 2002.

Kuhn, David P. *The Hardhat Riot: Nixon, New York City, and the Dawn of the White Working-Class Revolution*. New York: Oxford University Press, 2020.

Kunstler, James H. *The Geography of Nowhere: The Rise and Decline of America's Man-Made Landscape*. New York: Simon and Schuster, 1993.

LaBudde, Besse Freeman, et al. *Angel Mounds: A Mississippian Town on the Ohio River*. Evansville, IN: Friends of Angel Mounds, 2011.

Lane, Barbara M. *Houses for a New World: Builders and Buyers in American Suburbs, 1945–1965*. Princeton, NJ: Princeton University Press, 2015.

Lang, Robert E., and Rebecca R. Sohmer. "Legacy of the Housing Act of 1949: The Past, Present, and Future of Federal Housing and Urban Policy." *Housing Policy Debate* 11, no. 2 (January 2000): 291–98.

Lannert, Hallie B. *The Evansville Courier, Evansville, Indiana: Documenting a Century of Progress, 1845–1945*. Evansville, IN: Evansville Courier, 1945.

Lannert, Hallie, and Fred Foster. "Witnesses Face Contempt Citations. Refuse to Answer Questions as UE-CIO Red Inquiry Opens." *EC*, August 11, 1948.

Laprade, William T. "Academic Freedom and Tenure: Evansville College." *Bulletin of the American Association of University Professors* 35, no. 1 (Spring 1949): 74–111.

Leach, Chuck. "Commissioners Back Golf Plan." *EC*, March 31, 1970.

———. "Officials Alerted to Cope with Possible Violence." *EC*, May 9, 1974.

———. "Shooting of Couple Denied." *EC*, October 23, 1974.

———. "2 More Boys Face Charges." *EC*, August 2, 1968.

Levy, Peter B. *America in the Sixties—Right, Left, and Center: A Documentary History*. Santa Monica, CA: Praeger, 1998.

Lincolnshire Covenant. Evansville, IN: City of Evansville, 1923.

Loesch, Sarah. "'They Just Keep Pushing Us Poor Folks Around': From Villa Sites to Woodland Park." *ECP*, November 1, 2021.

Loewen, James W. *Sundown Towns: A Hidden Dimension of American Racism*. New York: New Press, 2018.

Longest, Dave. "'Monster Molders' Thrive in Local Plastics Industry." *SCP*, August 16, 1970.

LST 325: Workhorse of the Waves & Evansville's War Machine, 1942–45. Evansville, IN: Evansville Courier and Press, 2005.

MacLeod, Eilidh. Personal interview. Evansville, March 17, 2021.

MacLeod, James L. *The Cartoons of Evansville's Karl Kae Knecht: Half a Century of Artistic Activism*. Charleston, SC: The History Press, 2017.

———. *Evansville in World War II*. Charleston, SC: The History Press, 2015.

Madison, James H. *Hoosiers: A New History of Indiana*. Bloomington: Indiana University Press, 2014.

———. *The Indiana Way: A State History*. Bloomington: Indiana University Press, 1990.

———. *The Ku Klux Klan in the Heartland*. Bloomington: Indiana University Press, 2020.

Martin, John. "Business Leaders Honored." *ECP*, March 13, 2015.

Martin v. Evansville-Vanderburgh Sch. Corp., Indiana. U.S. District Court for the Southern District of Indiana - 347 F. Supp. 816 (S.D. Ind. September 5, 1972), 1972.

Marwick, Arthur. *The New Nature of History: Knowledge, Evidence, Language*. Chicago: Lyceum, 2001.

Marynell, Herb. "For Most, Relocation Has Happy Ending." *Sunday Courier*, July 17, 1988.

Massey, Douglas S., and Jonathan Tannen. "Suburbanization and Segregation in the United States: 1970–2010." *Ethnic and Racial Studies* 41, no. 9 (2017): 1,594–611.

Matthews, Garrett. "Depression Teaches Perspective—Those Who Lived Through It Reflect." *ECP*, November 27, 2008.

McBain, Roger. "Looking into the Past. Preservation: Her Passion, Her Work." *EP*, May 24, 1986.

———. "Shipyard Pictures Could Refocus Memories of War." *EC*, January 12, 1989.

McCabe, Thomas B. *The Committee for Economic Development—Its Past, Present, and Future*. New York: Committee for Economic Development, 1949.

McConnaughay, Dale. "Anguished Bosse Principal Searching for a Solution." *EP*, September 28, 1974.

McCutchan, Kenneth P. *From Then Til Now: History of McCutchanville*. Indianapolis: Indiana Historical Society, 1969.

McCutchan, Kenneth P., William E. Bartelt and Thomas R. Lonnberg. *Evansville at the Bend in the River: An Illustrated History*. American Historical Press, 2004.

McManus, Jane. "Moslem Life Workshop Teaches Educators about Islamic Faith." *EP*, October 2, 1995.

Melchior, D.S. *Legacy of War: Profiles of the 67 Brave Young Men from Evansville, IN Who Perished in the Vietnam War*. Bloomington, IN: iUniverse, 2008.

Mellon, Steve, and Donald E. Baker. *Evansville Then and Now*. Evansville, IN: Scripps Howard Publishing, 1995.

Meredith, Kathie. "Razing Project to Start Soon." *EP*, April 10, 1968, 11.

Miller, Milford M. "Evansville Steamboats During the Civil War." *Indiana Magazine of History* 37, no. 4 (December 1941): 359–81.

Mills, Randy. "'The Real Violence at Evansville': The Firing of Professor George F. Parker." *Indiana Magazine of History* 99, no. 2 (June 2003): 129–54.

Mills, Randy K., and Roxanne Mills. *Summer Wind: A Soldier's Road from Indiana to Vietnam*. Indianapolis: Blue River Press, 2017.

———. *Unexpected Journey: A Marine Corps Reserve Company in the Korean War*. Annapolis, MD: Naval Institute Press, 2000.

Minnis, Paul. "Prostitution in Evansville: Looking for Trouble." *EP*, July 29, 1996.

Mohl, Raymond A. "The Interstates and the Cities: The U.S. Department of Transportation and the Freeway Revolt, 1966–1973." *Journal of Policy History* 20, no. 2 (2008): 193–94.

———. "Stop the Road. Freeway Revolts in American Cities." *Journal of Urban History* 30, no. 5 (July 2004): 674–76.

Morgan, Harold B. *Home Front Heroes: Evansville and the Tri-State in WWII.* Evansville, IN: MT Publishing, 2007.

———. *Home Front Soldiers: Evansville and the Tri-State in World War II.* Evansville, IN: MT Publishing, 2015.

———. *Home Front Warriors: Building the P-47 Thunderbolt and the LST Warship in Evansville, Indiana During World War II.* Evansville, IN: MT Publishing, 2016.

———. *Home Town History: The Evansville, Indiana Area; A Photo Timeline.* Evansville, IN: Harold Morgan, 2009.

———. "Tri-State's War Effort Was Impressive and Varied." *ECP*, January 5, 2005.

Morgan, William. "Evansville: Smaller Version of Louisville." *SCP*, February 26, 1978.

Morlock, James E. *The Evansville Story: A Cultural Interpretation.* Evansville, IN: N.p., 1956.

———. "Wesselman Park and Nature Preserve. How Civic Appreciation Saved a Rare Downstate Property." *Outdoor Indiana*, July/August 1978, 12-18.

Moxley, Donovan, and Burnell Fischer. "Historic HOLC Redlining in Indianapolis and the Legacy of Environmental Impacts." *Journal of Public and Environmental Affairs* 1, no. 1 (April 2020).

Nickles, Shelley. "'Preserving Women': Refrigerator Design as Social Process in the 1930s." *Technology and Culture* 43, no. 4 (October 2002): 693–727.

O'Connor, Thomas H. *Building a New Boston: Politics and Urban Renewal, 1950–1970.* Lebanon, NH: University Press of New England, 1995.

Official Program and Souvenir of the Thirty-Seventh Annual Encampment of the Department of Indiana, Grand Army of the Republic. Evansville, IN: Evansville Ben Franklin Club, 1916.

Ogletree, Charles J. *All Deliberate Speed: Reflections on the First Half-Century of Brown v. Board of Education.* New York: W.W. Norton & Company, 2005.

Olmsted, Ralph. *From Institute to University.* Evansville, IN: University of Evansville, 1973.

Our Story: Once the Door Opened. Directed by Aaron Turner. 2021. Evansville: Aaroturn Productions, Film.

Pampe, Anne. "Local Open Housing Ordinance Passed. City Court Gets Jurisdiction." *EC*, November 19, 1968.

———. "Open Housing Measure Aired." *EC*, September 24, 1968.

———. "Open Housing Ordinance Planned by City Officials." *EC*, September 7, 1968.

Patry, Robert P. *City of the Four Freedoms: A History of Evansville, Indiana, a Survey of the History, Architectural Structures, and Personalities of Evansville, Indiana.* Friends of Willard Library, 1996.

Penland, Lynn R. "About Old North United Methodist Church." Old North UMC. Last modified August 14, 2016. https://oldnorthumc.com/about-onumc/.

Perkins, Janice. "Expressway Routing Okayed. Location on Division Gets Go Sign." *EC*, March 26, 1965.

———. "Governor, Sen. Hartke Guests for Dedication." *EC*, May 22, 1969.

———. "Housing Ordinance Amendments Urged." *EC*, October 3, 1968.

———. "Legal Action Authorized. Renewal Area Eviction Slated." *EC*, October 22, 1968.

———. "Local Public Housing Director Tells of 28-Year Career." *EC*, November 27, 1970.

Petroski, Henry. *The Road Taken: The History and Future of America's Infrastructure.* New York: Bloomsbury Publishing, 2016.

Pietila, Antero. *Not in My Neighborhood: How Bigotry Shaped a Great American City.* Chicago: Ivan R. Dee, 2010.

Poletika, Nicole. "Works Progress Administration Photographs, CA. 1936–1943." Indiana Historical Society. Last modified December 16, 2011. https://indianahistory.org/wp-content/uploads/wpa-photographs.pdf.

Pratt, Bob. "Gala Ribbon-Cutting Opens New Overpass." *EC*, March 21, 1956.

Prial, Frank J. "Charles H. King, 66; Conducted Seminars on Racial Attitudes." *New York Times*, September 17, 1991.

Rafford, Claire. "The 10 Most Endangered Properties in Indiana." *ECP*, August 23, 2022, 1, 5.

Reece, Clyde L. *Who's Who in Evansville ... Containing Biographies of Prominent Men and Women of Evansville, Indiana.* Evansville, IN: Burkert-Walton Company, 1932.

Rees, Jonathan. *Refrigeration Nation: A History of Ice, Appliances, and Enterprise in America.* Baltimore: JHU Press, 2013.

Reflections Upon a Century of Architecture, Evansville, Indiana. Evansville, IN: Junior League of Evansville, 1977.

A Resolution Memorializing the 50th Anniversary of the Passage of the City of Evansville Open Housing Ordinance. Evansville, IN: Common Council of the City of Evansville, 2018.

Robertson, Bill. "Overflow Crowd Sees Globetrotters' Basketball Circus Open New Stadium." October 29, 1956.

Rogers, Elie. "Indian City Evansville's First Subdivision Yields Clues to an Earlier Age." *SCP*, August 17, 1958.

Roll Call: The Military Aspect of Evansville in the Civil War. Evansville, IN: Vanderburgh County Historical Society, 2011.

Rome, Adam. *The Bulldozer in the Countryside: Suburban Sprawl and the Rise of American Environmentalism*. Cambridge: Cambridge University Press, 2001.

Rothstein, Richard. *The Color of Law: A Forgotten History of How Our Government Segregated America*. New York: Liveright Publishing, 2018.

Runge, Mel. "Bar Group Will Give Housing Law Opinion." *EP*, October 22, 1968.

———. "Clergymen Call for City-Enforced Open Housing." *EP*, October 18, 1968.

———. "Golf Course Proposed for Angel Mounds." *EP*, May 18, 1964.

———. "Question of City Ordinance on Open Housing Debated." *EP*, June 16, 1967.

———. "Young Negroes Heckle Candidate: Fights Flare." *EP*, October 10, 1968.

Rutan, Devin Q. "Legacies of the Residential Security Maps: Measuring the Persistent Effects of Redlining in Pittsburgh, Pennsylvania." Master's thesis, University of Pittsburgh, 2016.

Ryder, Tom. "Standing Room Only as Last of Brewery Is Razed." *EP*, June 25, 1965.

Schleper, Charles. "Citizenry Obeys, Applauds Curfew." *EP*, August 26, 1968.

———. "8-to-5 Curfew Imposed on City after Night of Racial Disorder. Business Burns, Policeman Shot." *EP*, August 24, 1968.

———. "Police Cruiser and 7 Other Cars Damaged by Rocks in Negro Area." *EP*, August 23, 1968.

Schlepper, Anne. "Peace Rally Draws 300." *EC*, May 9, 1970.

Schmitt, Stan. "Civic Duty." *Evansville Living*, July 3, 2019.

Schrader, Bill. "Building Wreckers Show New Concept in Civic Project." *SCP*, February 28, 1965.

Schwartz, Gary T. "Urban Freeways and the Interstate System." *Transportation Law Journal* 8 (1976): 167–264.

Seibert, Isaiah. "LST 325 Welcomed to New Downtown Evansville Home." *ECP*, June 13, 2020.

Seits, L.D. "Bull Island: It Ended an Era and Two Lives, but Changed Some Futures Too." *EP*, August 30, 1982.

Sievers, Fred. "Civic Center Construction Under Way," *EP*, June 20, 1966.

Small, Andrew. "The Wastelands of Urban Renewal." CityLab, last modified February 14, 2017, https://www.citylab.com/equity/2017/02/urban-renewal-wastelands/516378/.

Snepp, Daniel W. *Sidelights of Early Evansville History*. Evansville, IN: Privately published, 1976.

Snow, Dean R., Nancy Gonlin and Peter E. Siegel. *The Archaeology of Native North America*. London: Routledge, 2019.

Spachner, Esther. "Residents of Villa Sites Area Live in Squalor, But Keep Pride." *EC*, October 17, 1955.

Sprinkles, Dallas W. *The History of Evansville Blacks*. Evansville, IN: Mid-America Enterprises, 1973.

Stanton, Betsy. "Veterans Day: Making Peace with Memories." *EC*, November 6, 1987.

Steigerwald, David. *The Sixties and the End of Modern America*. New York: St Martin's Press, 1995.

Stems, Suzanne. "Wesselman Park Planned as All-Recreation Area." *EC*, September 24, 1963.

Stern, Douglas L., and Joan Marchand. "Oak Hill Cemetery History." City of Evansville. Accessed June 22, 2022. https://www.evansvillegov.org/city/topic/index.php?topicid=964&structureid=67.

———. United States Department of the Interior Heritage Conservation and Recreation Service National Register Of Historic Places Inventory—Nomination Form. Evansville, 1981.

Stout, Wesley W. *Bullets by the Billion*. Detroit, MI : Chrysler Corporation, 1946.

Suarez-Villa, Luis. "Regional Inversion in the United States: The Institutional Context for the Rise of the Sunbelt since the 1940s." *Tijdschrift voor economische en sociale geografie* 93, no. 4 (2002): 424–42.

Swanson, Patricia. "Black Activist Recalls Evansville Pastorate." *EP*, March 2, 1983.

Thornbrough, Emma L. *Indiana Blacks in the Twentieth Century*. Bloomington: Indiana University Press, 2000.

Townsend, Paul. "Interstate 64 Battle Continues." *EC*, March 26, 1960.

———. "Whirlpool Gets Servel Appliances," *EC*, January 4, 1958.

Tsai, Mau S. *The Development of the Evansville Regional Economy from 1945 to 1970*. Evansville, IN: University of Evansville, 1972.

Tucker, Kristen. "70 Years of Master Plans." *Evansville Living*, January 20, 2016.

25 Years of Community Redevelopment Progress, Evansville, Indiana, 1954–1979. Evansville, IN, 1980.

Uselton, George, and Dick Densley. "Vandals Hurl Firebombs at Central." *EC*, April 16, 1968.

Vanderburgh County: Interim Report. Indianapolis: Historic Landmarks Foundation of Indiana, 1994.

Ventry, Dennis J., Jr. "The Accidental Deduction. A History and Critique of the Tax Subsidy for Mortgage Interest." *Law and Contemporary Problems* 73, no. 233 (Winter 2010): 233–84.

Vinen, Richard. *1968: Radical Protest and Its Enemies.* New York: Harper, 2018.

Wallace, Phil. "Parents Planning Whites-Only School." *EC*, August 14, 1972.

Wallis, Jim. *America's Original Sin: Racism, White Privilege, and the Bridge to a New America.* Grand Rapids, MI: Brazos Press, 2016.

Ward, Brian. *The 1960s: A Documentary Reader.* Hoboken, NJ: Wiley-Blackwell, 2009.

Wathen, Patrick W. "August 14, 1945 War's End Evansville Joined National Party." *ECP*, August 14, 1995.

———. "Evansville Needs Grand Reminder of Its Efforts During War." *ECP*, August 27, 1995.

———. "Integration Specialist Arrested after Melee." *EC*, September 21, 1974.

———. "Rights Official Believes Gunmen Not the Same." *EC*, May 6, 1974.

———. "Twenty Arrested at Rockfest on Drug, Disorderly Charges." *EC*, July 2, 1973.

———. "WNIN's 'War Stories' Shares Local Experiences." *ECP*, August 17, 1995.

Weber, Joe. "Yesterday's Freeway Network of Tomorrow." *Geographical Review* 106, no. 1 (January 2016): 54–71.

"'We Don't Intend to Fall In Anymore at the End of the Parade.'" *Indiana Historian*, February 1995, 1–16.

"The Week in Review." *People's Voice* 1, no. 1 (October 1970).

Welky, David. *The Thousand-Year Flood: The Ohio-Mississippi Disaster of 1937.* Chicago: University of Chicago Press, 2011.

Wersich, Carol. "Lincoln Gardens' Demise Will Be Marked." *ECP*, December 4, 1997.

———. "LST Production Lines Brought Boom Times to Evansville—an Economic Shot in the Arm." *ECP*, July 14, 2003.

White, Edward, and Robert D. Owen. *Evansville and Its Men of Mark.* Evansville, IN: Evansville Journal Company, 1873.

White, Samuel W. *Fragile Alliances: Labor and Politics in Evansville, Indiana, 1919–1955*. Santa Barbara, CA: Greenwood Publishing Group, 2005.

———. "Popular Anticommunism and the UE in Evansville, Indiana." In *American Labor and the Cold War. Grassroots Politics and Postwar Culture*, 141–53. New Brunswick, NJ: Rutgers University Press, 2004.

Whitham, Charlie. "The Committee for Economic Development, Foreign Trade and the Rise of American Corporate Liberalism, 1942–8." *Journal of Contemporary History* 48, no. 4 (2013): 845–71. doi:10.1177/0022009413493944.

Wilkinson, William C., Jr. "Memories of the Ku Klux Klan in One Indiana Town." *Indiana Magazine of History* 102 (December 2006): 339–54.

Willard Library and Evansville Zoological Society. *A Pictorial History of Mesker Park Zoo*. Evansville, IN: MT Publishing, 2011.

Williams, H.F. *Your Career Opportunities in Evansville Industry*. Evansville, IN: Evansville Manufactures and Employers Association Public Relations Division, 1953.

Williams, Juan. *Eyes on the Prize: America's Civil Rights Years, 1954–1965*. New York: Penguin, 2013.

Wilson, Mark. "Civil Rights Leader Dies." *ECP*, September 22, 2020.

———. "Tale of Two Highways." *ECP*, December 8, 2002.

Wilson, William E. "Long, Hot Summer in Indiana." *American Heritage* 16, no. 5 (1965).

Wiltse, Jeff. *Contested Waters: A Social History of Swimming Pools in America*. Chapel Hill: University of North Carolina Press, 2007.

Wolcott, Victoria W. "The Forgotten History of Segregated Swimming Pools and Amusement Parks." The Conversation. Last modified July 9, 2019. https://theconversation.com/the-forgotten-history-of-segregated-swimming-pools-and-amusement-parks-119586.

Wood, Amy L. *Lynching and Spectacle: Witnessing Racial Violence in America, 1890–1940*. Chapel Hill: University of North Carolina Press, 2009.

Worthy, William. *The Rape of Our Neighborhoods: And How Communities Are Resisting Take-Overs by Colleges, Hospitals, Churches, Businesses, and Public Agencies*. New York: Morrow, 1976.

Wright, Guy. "Mild 'Little' Meeting on Public Housing Becomes Red Hot." *EP*, December 7, 1949.

Zelizer, Julian E. *The Fierce Urgency of Now: Lyndon Johnson, Congress, and the Battle for the Great Society*. London: Penguin, 2015.

INDEX

ABOUT THE AUTHOR

Photo by Jessica MacLeod.

James Lachlan MacLeod was educated at the University of Edinburgh in Scotland, and is Professor of History and Department Chair at the University of Evansville. He is the author of three books: *The Second Disruption*, *Evansville in World War II*, and *The Cartoons of Evansville's Karl Kae Knecht*. He serves on various boards locally and in 2021 he received the Indiana Historical Society's Hubert Hawkins History Award in recognition of his distinguished service and career in local history.